821.4 Joh

John Milton /

cyf $0.00
34028049529838   ocm49991425

Bloom's BioCritiques

Dante Alighieri
Maya Angelou
Jane Austen
The Brontë Sisters
Lord Byron
Geoffrey Chaucer
Anton Chekhov
Stephen Crane
Emily Dickinson
William Faulkner
F. Scott Fitzgerald
Robert Frost
Ernest Hemingway
Langston Hughes
Stephen King
Arthur Miller
John Milton
Toni Morrison
Edgar Allan Poe
J. D. Salinger
William Shakespeare
John Steinbeck
Mark Twain
Alice Walker
Walt Whitman
Tennessee Williams

Bloom's BioCritiques

JOHN MILTON

Edited and with an introduction by
Harold Bloom
Sterling Professor of the Humanities
Yale University

Philadelphia

©2003 by Chelsea House Publishers, a subsidiary of
Haights Cross Communications.

A Haights Cross Communications Company

Introduction © 2003 by Harold Bloom.

All rights reserved. No part of this publication may be
reproduced or transmitted in any form or by any means
without the written permission of the publisher.

Printed and bound in the United States of America

10 9 8 7 6 5 4 3 2 1

Library of Congress Cataloging-in-Publication Data

John Milton / editor, Harold Bloom ; contributing editor, Neil Heims.
    p. cm. — (Bloom's biocritiques)
Includes bibliographical references and index.
  ISBN 0-7910-6370-4
  1. Milton, John, 1608-1674—Criticism and interpretation. I. Bloom,
Harold. II. Heims, Neil. III. Series.
  PR3588 .J653 2002
  821'.4—dc21
                                2002009107

Chelsea House Publishers
1974 Sproul Road, Suite 400
Broomall, PA 19008-0914

http://www.chelseahouse.com

Contributing editor: Neil Heims

Cover image © Hutton Getty/Liaison Agency

Cover design by Keith Trego

Layout by EJB Publishing Services

Contents

User's Guide   vii

The Work in the Writer   ix
   Harold Bloom

Introduction   1
   Harold Bloom

Biography of John Milton   7
   Ellyn Sanna

Milton: An Introduction   35
   Neil Heims

On Poetry and Poets   57
   T. S. Eliot

The Interpretative Choice   81
   Stanley Eugene Fish

Paradise Regained and the Politics of Martyrdom   111
   Laura Lunger Knoppers

Chronology   135

Works by John Milton   137

Works about John Milton   139

Contributors   145

Index   147

User's Guide

These volumes are designed to introduce the reader to the life and work of the world's literary masters. Each volume begins with Harold Bloom's essay "The Work in the Writer" and a volume-specific introduction also written by Professor Bloom. Following these unique introductions is an engaging biography that discusses the major life events and important literary accomplishments of the author under consideration.

Furthermore, each volume includes an original critique that not only traces the themes, symbols, and ideas apparent in the author's works, but strives to put those works into a cultural and historical perspective. In addition to the original critique is a brief selection of significant critical essays previously published on the author and his or her works followed by a concise and informative chronology of the writer's life. Finally, each volume concludes with a bibliography of the writer's works, a list of additional readings, and an index of important themes and ideas.

HAROLD BLOOM

The Work in the Writer

Literary biography found its masterpiece in James Boswell's *Life of Samuel Johnson*. Boswell, when he treated Johnson's writings, implicitly commented upon Johnson as found in his work, even as in the great critic's life. Modern instances of literary biography, such as Richard Ellmann's lives of W. B. Yeats, James Joyce, and Oscar Wilde, essentially follow in Boswell's pattern.

That the writer somehow is in the work, we need not doubt, though with William Shakespeare, writer-of-writers, we almost always need to rely upon pure surmise. The exquisite rancidities of the Problem Plays or Dark Comedies seem to express an extraordinary estrangement of Shakespeare from himself. When we read or attend *Troilus and Cressida* and *Measure for Measure*, we may be startled by particular speeches of Ulysses in the first play, or of Vincentio in the second. These speeches, of Ulysses upon hierarchy or upon time, or of Duke Vincentio upon death, are too strong either for their contexts or for the characters of their speakers. The same phenomenon occurs with Parolles, the military impostor of *All's Well That Ends Well*. Utterly disgraced, he nevertheless affirms: "Simply the thing I am/Shall make me live."

In Shakespeare, more even than in his peers, Dante and Cervantes, meaning always starts itself again through excess or overflow. The strongest of Shakespeare's creatures—Falstaff, Hamlet, Iago, Lear, Cleopatra—have an exuberance that is fiercer than their plays can contain. If Ben Jonson was at all correct in his complaint that "Shakespeare wanted art," it could have been only in a sense that he may not have intended. Where do the personalities of Falstaff or Hamlet touch a limit? What was it in Shakespeare that made the two parts of *Henry IV* and *Hamlet* into "plays unlimited"? Neither Falstaff nor Hamlet will be stopped: their wit, their beautiful, laughing speech, their intensity of being—all these are virtually infinite.

In what ways do Falstaff and Hamlet manifest the writer in the work? Evidently, we can never know, or know enough to answer with any authority. But what would happen if we reversed the question, and asked: How did the work form the writer, Shakespeare?

Of Shakespeare's inwardness, his biography tells us nothing. And yet, to an astonishing extent, Shakespeare created our inwardness. At the least, we can speculate that Shakespeare so lived his life as to conceal the depths of his nature, particularly as he rather prematurely aged. We do not have Shakespeare on Shakespeare, as any good reader of the Sonnets comes to realize: they do not constitute a key that unlocks his heart. No sequence of sonnets could be less confessional or more powerfully detached from the poet's self.

The German poet and universal genius, Goethe, affords a superb contrast to Shakespeare. Of Goethe's life, we know more than everything; I wonder sometimes if we know as much about Napoleon or Freud or any other human being who ever has lived, as we know about Goethe. Everywhere, we can find Goethe in his work, so much so that Goethe seems to crowd the writing out, just as Byron and Oscar Wilde seem to usurp their own literary accomplishments. Goethe, cunning beyond measure, nevertheless invested a rival exuberance in his greatest works that could match his personal charisma. The sublime outrageousness of the Second Part of *Faust*, or of the greater lyric and meditative poems, form a Counter-Sublime to Goethe's own daemonic intensity.

Goethe was fascinated by the daemonic in himself; we can doubt that Shakespeare had any such interests. Evidently, Shakespeare abandoned his acting career just before he composed *Measure for Measure* and *Othello*. I surmise that the egregious interventions by Vincentio and Iago displace the actor's energies into a new kind of mischief-making, a fresh opening to a subtler playwriting-within-the-play.

But what had opened Shakespeare to this new awareness? The answer is the work in the writer, *Hamlet* in Shakespeare. One can go further: it was not so much the play, *Hamlet*, as the character Hamlet, who changed Shakespeare's art forever.

Hamlet's personality is so large and varied that it rivals Goethe's own. Ironically Goethe's Faust, his Hamlet, has no personality at all, and is as colorless as Shakespeare himself seems to have chosen to be. Yet nothing could be more colorful than the Second Part of *Faust*, which is peopled by an astonishing array of monsters, grotesque devils, and classical ghosts.

A contrast between Shakespeare and Goethe demonstrates that in each—but in very different ways—we can better find the work in the person, than we can discover that banal entity, the person in the work. Goethe to many of his contemporaries, seemed to be a mortal god. Shakespeare, so far as we know, seemed an affable, rather ordinary fellow, who aged early and became somewhat withdrawn. Yet Faust, though Mephistopheles battles for his soul, is hardly worth the trouble unless you take him as an idea and not as a person. Hamlet is nearly every-idea-in-one, but he is precisely a personality and a person.

Would Hamlet be so astonishingly persuasive if his father's ghost did not haunt him? Falstaff is more alive than Prince Hal, who says that the devil haunts him in the shape of an old fat man. Three years before composing the final *Hamlet*, Shakespeare invented Falstaff, who then never ceased to haunt his creator. Falstaff and Hamlet may be said to best represent the work in the writer, because their influence upon Shakespeare was prodigious. W.H. Auden accurately observed that Falstaff possesses infinite energy: never tired, never bored, and absolutely both witty and happy until Hal's rejection destroys him. Hamlet too has infinite energy, but in him it is more curse than blessing.

Falstaff and Hamlet can be said to occupy the roles in Shakespeare's invented world that Sancho Panza and Don Quixote possess in Cervantes's. Shakespeare's plays from 1610 on (starting with *Twelfth Night*) are thus analogous to the Second Part of Cervantes's epic novel. Sancho and the Don overtly jostle Cervantes for authorship in the Second Part, even as Cervantes battles against the impostor who has pirated a continuation of his work. As a dramatist, Shakespeare manifests the work in the writer more indirectly. Falstaff's prose genius is revived in the scapegoating of Malvolio by Maria and Sir Toby Belch, while Falstaff's darker insights are developed by Feste's melancholic wit. Hamlet's intellectual resourcefulness, already deadly, becomes poisonous in Iago and in Edmund. Yet we have not crossed into the deeper abysses of the work in the writer in later Shakespeare.

No fictive character, before or since, is Falstaff's equal in self-trust. Sir John, whose delight in himself is contagious, has total confidence both in his self-awareness and in the resources of his language. Hamlet, whose self is as strong, and whose language is as copious, nevertheless distrusts both the self and language. Later Shakespeare is, as it were, much under the influence both of Falstaff and of Hamlet, but they tug him in opposite directions. Shakespeare's own copiousness of language is well-nigh incredible: a vocabulary in excess of twenty-one thousand words, almost eighteen hundred of which he coined himself. And of his word-hoard, nearly half are used only once each, as though the perfect setting for each had been found, and need not be repeated. Love for language and faith in language are Falstaffian attributes. Hamlet will darken both that love and that faith in Shakespeare, and perhaps the Sonnets can best be read as Falstaff and Hamlet counterpointing against one another.

Can we surmise how aware Shakespeare was of Falstaff and Hamlet, once they had played themselves into existence? *Henry IV, Part I* appeared in six quarto editions during Shakespeare's lifetime; *Hamlet* possibly had four. Falstaff and Hamlet were played again and again at the Globe, but Shakespeare knew also that they were being read, and he must have had contact with some of those readers. What would it have been like to discuss Falstaff or Hamlet with one of their early readers (presumably also part of their audience at the Globe), if you were the creator of such demiurges? The question would seem nonsensical to most Shakespeare scholars, but then these days they tend to be either ideologues or moldy figs. How can we recover the uncanniness of Falstaff and of Hamlet, when they now have become so familiar?

A writer's influence upon himself is an unexplored problem in criticism, but such an influence is never free from anxieties. The biocritical problem (which this series attempts to explore) can be divided into two areas, difficult to disengage fully. Accomplished works affect the author's life, and also affect her subsequent writings. It is simpler for me to surmise the effect of *Mrs. Dalloway* and *To the Lighthouse* upon Woolf's late *Between the Acts*, than it is to relate Clarissa Dalloway's suicide and Lily Briscoe's capable endurance in art to the tragic death and complex life of Virginia Woolf.

There are writers whose lives were so vivid that they seem sometimes to obscure the literary achievement: Byron, Wilde, Malraux, Hemingway. But most major Western writers do not live that exuberantly, and the greatest of all, Shakespeare, sometimes appears to have adopted the personal mask of colorlessness. And yet there are heroes of literature who struggled titanically with their own eras—Tolstoy, Milton, Victor Hugo—who nevertheless matter more for their works than their lives.

There are great figures—Emily Dickinson, Wallace Stevens, Willa Cather—who seem to have had so little of the full intensity of life when compared to the vitality of their work, that we might almost speak of the work in the work, rather than even of the work in a person. Emily Brontë might well be the extreme instance of such a visionary, surpassing William Blake in that one regard.

I conclude this general introduction to a series of literary bio-critiques by stating a tentative formula or principle for gauging the many ways in which the work influences the person and her subsequent, later work. Our influence upon ourselves is always related to the Shakespearean invention of self-overhearing, which I have written about in several other contexts. Life, as well as poetry and prose, is overheard rather than simply heard. The writer listens to herself as though she were somebody else, and the will to change begins to operate. The forces that live in us include the prior work we have done, and the dreams and waking visions that evade our dismissals.

HAROLD BLOOM

Introduction

After Shakespeare and Chaucer, John Milton is the most eminent poet in the English language. Since he is an immensely learned poet, Milton becomes increasingly difficult for most readers at a time when we are less deeply educated than many of us were in the past. After a half-century at Yale University, I am aware that no one remarks to me of a colleague that she or he is remarkably "learned." Erudition is hardly in fashion.

John Milton may be the most radical instance I know of the work in a writer, or the influence of an exemplary mind upon itself. No other great poet, even Dante, began with so clear and systematic an intention to devote himself entirely to poetry, with the ambition of surpassing all forerunners. And no other major poet ever has read so deeply and extensively as Milton did. He desired a life cloistered but secular, in which poetry and learning, fused together, were to be his central preoccupations. Until he was thirty-three, he lived his dream, at Cambridge University, and at Horton, his father's country estate near Windsor, and then in a long Italian tour in 1638-1639. From 1640 on, he lived in London, teaching at his own school, and continuing his preparation for epic accomplishment.

The struggle against the monarchy and its bishops began, for Milton, in 1641, when he took the side of Protestantism and Parliament in the gathering conflict that led to the English Civil War. For twenty years—before, during, and after his service to Cromwell and the Commonwealth as Secretary for Foreign Tongues to the Council of State—Milton devoted his creative energies to polemical prose tracts.

Let us begin by looking at Milton's poetry up through 1637, when it culminated in *Lycidas*, a year before his Italian tour. His greatness is first manifested in *L'Allegro* and *Il Penseroso*, matched extended lyrics in tetrameter couplets that still retain their extraordinary freshness and originality. Immensely playful, they resonate with intimations of a giant art to come:

> Lap me in soft Lydian airs,
> Married to immortal verse,
> Such as the meeting soul may pierce
> In notes with many a winding bout
> Of linked sweetness long drawn out,
> With wanton heed and giddy cunning,
> The melting voice through mazes running,
> Untwisting all the chains that tie
> The hidden soul of harmony;
> That Orpheus' self may heave his head
> From golden slumber on a bed
> Of heaped Elysian flowers, and hear
> Such strains as would have won the ear
> Of Pluto, to have quite set free
> His half-regained Eurydice.
> These delights if thou canst give,
> Mirth, with thee I mean to live.

This conclusion might be called Milton's Song of Innocence, to be contrasted with the close of *Il Penseroso* as a Song of Experience:

> There let the pealing organ blow
> To the full-voiced quire below,
> In service high and anthems clear,
> As may with sweetness, through mine ear,
> Dissolve me into ecstasies,
> And bring all heaven before mine eyes.
> And may at last my weary age
> Find out the peaceful hermitage,
> The hairy gown and mossy cell,
> Where I may sit and rightly spell
> Of every star that heaven doth shew,

> And every herb that sips the dew,
> Till old experience do attain
> To something like prophetic strain.
> These pleasures, Melancholy, give,
> And I with thee will choose to live.

This is Milton at twenty-three or twenty-four, sublimely picturing himself as a new Orpheus, with all the imaginative world still before him. In 1634, Milton's pastoral masque, *Comus*, with music by his friend Henry Lawes, was performed. It remains a work of enduring beauty, strongly influenced by Shakespeare's *A Midsummer Night's Dream*, *The Winter's Tale* and *The Tempest*. So astonishing was the young Milton's artistry that *Comus* is able to absorb Shakespeare at his pastoral perfection without being destroyed by this strongest of precursors.

The culmination of Milton's early poetry is *Lycidas*, the superb pastoral elegy written when the poet was twenty-nine, soon after the death of his mother. *Lycidas*, an extended canzone of one hundred and ninety-three lines, is quite possibly the best shorter poem in the language, and is properly one of the most demanding. The true subject of *Lycidas* is neither Edward King, a young poet drowned in the Irish Sea, and a classmate of Milton at Cambridge, nor the evaded death of the mother. Rather, the poem contemplates Milton's dread of being cut off before he had time to compose the major poems he lived to write:

> Alas! What boots it with uncessant care
> To tend the homely slighted shepherd's trade,
> And strictly meditate the thankless Muse?
> Were it not better done as others use,
> To sport with Amaryllis in the shade,
> Or with the tangles of Neaera's hair?
> Fame is the spur that the clear spirit doth raise
> (That last infirmity of noble mind)
> To scorn delights, and love laborious days;
> But the fair guerdon when we hope to find,
> And think to burst out into sudden blaze,
> Comes the blind Fury with the abhorred shears,
> And slits the thin-spun life.

This did not happen, and Milton survived to write *Paradise Lost* (1658-1665), *Paradise Regained* (1667-1670), and *Samson Agonistes* (possibly 1670-1671). By 1652, in his mid-forties, Milton was completely blind. In 1660, the monarchy was restored: Milton's books were burned by the hangman in London, and the defiant poet was arrested and locked up from October to December. Fortunately, the government of Charles II released him, though he could have been hanged as a defender of regicide. When Milton died, in early November, 1674, he was just short of sixty-six. His personal life (three marriages, and three resentful daughters) had not been particularly happy, and his religious and political hopes for his nation had been destroyed, but *Paradise Lost* and *Samson Agonistes* were triumphant accomplishments, absolute fulfillments of his lifelong ambitions.

The influence of Milton's mind upon itself best can be conveyed, in my judgment, by bringing together portions of the four invocations to *Paradise Lost*, that commence Books I, III, VII, and IX of the only epic that can rival the *Iliad* and the *Odyssey*. I give a *cento* drawn from the invocations:

> And chiefly thou, O Spirit, that dost prefer
> Before all temples the upright heart and pure,
> Instruct me, for thou knowest; thou from the first
> Wast present, and with mighty wings outspread
> Dove-like sat'st brooding on the vast abyss
> And mad'st it pregnant: what in me is dark
> Illumine, what is low raise and support ... (I.17-23)

> Then feed on thoughts that voluntary move
> Harmonious numbers, as the wakeful bird
> Sings darkling, and in shadiest covert hid
> Tunes her nocturnal note. Thus with the year
> Seasons return; but not to me returns
> Day, or the sweet approach of even or morn,
> Or sight of vernal bloom, or summer's rose,
> Or flocks, or herds, or human face divine;
> But cloud instead, and ever-during dark
> Surrounds me, from the cheerful ways of men
> Cut off, and for the book of knowledge fair
> Presented with a universal blank

> Of Nature's works to me expunged and razed,
> And wisdom at one entrance quite shut out.
> So much the rather thou, celestial Light,
> Shine inward, and the mind through all her powers
> Irradiate, there plant eyes, all mist from thence
> Purge and disperse, that I may see and tell
> Of things invisible to mortal sight ... (III.37-55)

>   Up led by thee
> Into the heaven of heavens I have presumed,
> An earthly guest, and drawn empyreal air,
> Thy tempering; with like safety guided down,
> Return me to my native element ... (VII.12-16)

> If answerable style I can obtain
> Of my celestial patroness, who deigns
> Her nightly visitation unimplored,
> And dictates to me slumbering, or inspires
> Easy my unpremeditated verse,
> Since first this subject for heroic song
> Pleased me long choosing, and beginning late... (IX.20-26)

What Milton has taught Milton is the fruit of thirty years and more of profound meditation upon extraordinary learning and native genius. Not blindness, disgrace, imprisonment, or danger, or a life filled with marital and familial discord, has prevented a great consciousness from expanding to its limits. Milton more than earned the magnificent final line of *Samson Agonistes*:

And calm of mind, all passion spent.

ELLYN SANNA

Biography of John Milton

An Undying Ambition

John Milton was born in London on December 9, 1608. He was the elder son of the scrivener and composer, John Milton and his wife Sara. Milton's father wanted to provide his son with the best intellectual training he could afford. As a prosperous businessman in London, Milton's father could afford private tutors and later the best private schools, such as St. Paul's. From a young age, Milton was a gifted student, particularly of languages. He learned Latin and Greek, in addition to a number of European languages. Milton profited from the education he received, but later in life he criticized English schools. In *On Education*, he complained that schoolboys were tormented by being forced to learn the small details of Latin grammar rather than allowing them to enjoy the great works of the classical authors. Despite this curriculum, he managed to absorb a good deal of philosophical insight from the Greek and Latin authors he studied; his imagination was stimulated by the works of these great masters. His knowledge of the classics, along with studies in the Renaissance and Italian language, influenced his later writing style. Milton was very studious and an avid reader from his early years. He formed several enduring relationships with other boys who shared his interests in literature and learning. One of these boys was Charles Diodate, the son of an Italian Protestant refugee who had become a famous London doctor. For nearly 20 years, Charles Diodate was Milton's closest friend, the confidant with whom he discussed his hopes and sorrows.

By the time he was fifteen, Milton was already demonstrating his skill with words. He translated some of the Psalms from Latin into English verse, and he practiced writing in Latin as well. Latin was an essential language to anyone who wanted to communicate in writing to a large audience, since Latin was the universal language used by every branch of learning in the 17th century. However, English was becoming a more respected literary medium. Milton was born into an age of influential English creativity. The London of his day was filled with the language and poetry of John Donne, William Shakespeare, John Webster, Ben Jonson, and Edmund Spenser. Milton read and admired these great authors; they proved to him that the English language had just as much range for poetry and beauty as did Italian and the great classical languages.

Milton may have been ambitious, but even as a teenager he took his gifts seriously, considering them to be entrusted to him by God. Religious faith was a central part of his family's life, and Milton grew up with the idea that his career and life should be directed toward something bigger than merely selfish ambition. He dedicated his poetry to both God and his country's service and wrote that he wanted to be "himself a true poem, that is a composition and pattern of the best and honourablest things, not presuming to sing high praises of heroic men or famous cities unless he have himself the experience and practice of all that which is praiseworthy."

When Milton was about seventeen, he left St. Paul's school and went to Christ's College at Cambridge, where he had a difficult time with the pedagogical attitude. While St. Paul's had been progressive in its approach to learning, Cambridge focused on rigid, traditional education from the medieval period. The teaching was based on the medieval system of training in logic and argument, and Milton felt that this approach was irrelevant to the world in which he lived. He cared little about abstract intellectual exercises, and his mind frequently wandered from his studies. He wrote:

> Many a time, when the duty of tracing out these petty subtleties for a while has been laid upon me, when my mind has been dulled and my sight blurred by continual reading—many a time, I say, I have paused to take breath, and have sought some slight relief from my boredom in looking to see how much yet remained of my task. When, as always

happened, I found that more remained to be done than I had as yet got through, how often I have wished that instead of having these fooleries forced upon me I had been set to clean out the stable of Augeas again, and I have envied Hercules his luck in having been spared such labours as these by a kindly Juno.

Milton was not popular at Cambridge. His tutor did not like him, and neither did his teachers nor his fellow students. He was outspoken about his ideas for reforming education, which did not win him sympathy. However, he believed that education should be both more imaginative and more comprehensive.

Despite his impatience with his studies, Milton took advantage of his time at Cambridge to pursue his poetry. In 1625, during his first year at the university, he composed the elegy titled, "On the Death of a Fair Infant," a poem he wrote to comfort his sister Ann, who had just lost a baby. This early poem is considered to be more of a schoolboy's exercise than a great work of poetry, but in 1629, when he was 21, Milton proved he was maturing as a poet when he wrote "On the Morning of Christ's Nativity."

This poem was rich in imagery and full of verbal music; he achieved small fame from this poem and was asked to contribute a sonnet to the second folio edition of Shakespeare's plays. The sonnet he wrote illustrates the differences he perceived between himself as a poet and Shakespeare, the great bard. Shakespeare's poetry, Milton wrote, was full of "easy numbers" and "woodnotes wild," while his own work was "slow endeavoring art." Shakespeare's insights and talents, Milton recognized, had little to do with the book learning and intellectual pursuits that so fascinated Milton himself.

During the summer vacation of 1631, Milton wrote "L'Allegro" and "Il Penseroso," two pastoral poems that combined his classical background with his love for the English countryside. "L'Allegro" spoke of "Meadows trim with daisies pied, / Shallow brooks and rivers wide ...," while in "Il Penseroso" he described the sensuous delight of hushed, religious moments that "Dissolve me into ecstasies, / And bring all heaven before mine eyes...." Although Milton considered himself a Protestant, these poems had little in common with the austere and strict world of the Puritans.

During Milton's years at Cambridge, he was considering the Church as a career. His parents would have been pleased if he became a clergyman, and this was the obvious professional choice for a young man who was a gifted intellectual. However, he was shocked by the behavior of young men studying for ministry in the Anglican Church, and he was equally disturbed by the real-life ramifications of the Puritans' beliefs. The Anglican Church was in the midst of serious financial problems; anyone who became an Anglican minister needed to court a powerful and wealthy patron if he hoped to make a living, and this practice often led to corruption and a loss of ideals. Meanwhile, the Puritans faced political dangers if they expressed their beliefs openly. A close friend of Milton's, Alexander Gill, the son of the high master at St. Paul's, was in serious trouble for expressing an opinion at a private gathering. Gill was sentenced to pay a heavy fine, to stand in the pillory, and to lose both his ears. The harsh sentence was never carried out, but Gill's predicament was a sober warning to Milton and his other friends.

Many Puritans disliked the Church of England's structure. They believed that the Prayer Book was confining and should be done away with, so that churchgoers would rely only on Scripture for inspiration; these dissenters also wanted a more democratic system that included lay leaders and elected ministers. The tension within the church grew still stronger when King Charles I decided to strengthen the authority of the bishops and enforce a uniform ritual through the church. During Milton's time at Cambridge, angry Puritans in the House of Commons overpowered the Speaker and passed resolutions that defied the King's policies. Charles I imprisoned the outspoken Puritan leaders without a trial; he let it be know that in the future he would govern the country—and the Church—without Parliament's help. Milton's dissatisfaction with these contemporary religious affairs led him to consider a secular writing career instead.

YEARS OF PREPARATION

When Milton left Cambridge, he went to live with his parents, first in Hammersmith and then in Horton, small villages in the countryside not far from London. Milton spent the next five years working his way through an enormous reading program he had mapped out for himself. He planned to study world history from the very beginning, relying on all the authorities that were then known. The general knowledge he would gain from this reading, he believed, would give him the foundation needed to pursue a life of wisdom.

Although he was isolated during these years from the life he had known in London, Milton continued to correspond with his friend Charles Diodati, exchanging news and ideas. When Diodati complained that Milton did not visit more often, Milton wrote:

> Your method of study is, as I know, such as to allow of frequent breathing-spaces, visits to friends, a good deal of writing, and not infrequent journeys; while my disposition is such that no delay, no rest, no thought or care for anything else, can divert me from my purpose, until I reach my goal and complete some great cycle of my studies.

In another letter to Diodati Milton revealed the reason why his studies were so disciplined. "What am I thinking about, you ask," he wrote. "So help me God, of immortality. What am I doing? Growing wings and learning to fly." Milton's letter to his friend reveals the depth of his dedication and ambition. As he continued to study, his goal took on greater shape and form. But while he was developing his writing talents for his eventual opus, he wrote two long poems, *Comus*, and *Lycidas*.

Comus is a masque, a form of entertainment that was fashionable at the time. A masque was acted out on a stage; it usually had a theme, but it was generally little more than a vehicle for songs, dances, and pretty scenery. Anne of Denmark, the wife of King James I, had made the masque popular in her court, and it had spread from there to the nobility. Masques were often performed at weddings or other celebrations.

In 1634, when the Earl of Bridgewater was sent to govern the border of Wales, he had in his household a music master, Henry Lawes, who was also a friend of Milton's. Lawes decided to write a masque for the Earl's three children to perform, and he turned to Milton to supply the words.

Comus tells the story of a young girl who is lost in a dark forest. When Comus, the wild son of Circe and Bacchus, captures her, he tempts her to drink a magic potion that will put her forever in his power. She withstands his temptation, however, and is rescued by her two brothers. Lady Alice, the Earl's daughter, played the heroine's role; she was 15 at the time, while her brothers, who played her rescuers, were 11 and 9.

Milton's masque was a bit different from the others of his day, however, for *Comus* was not merely a light piece of frothy entertainment. The masque allegorizes the conflict between good and evil. Although Milton's words were lyrical and his story well-suited to the young performers and the family occasion, he nevertheless made this deeper meaning clear.

Three years later he was asked to contribute an elegy to a memorial planned by the friends of Edward King, a young Cambridge student who drowned soon after he was ordained for the ministry. Books of poetry written in honor of a departed friend or loved one were common in the 17th century, but the poem Milton contributed in Edward King's honor has made King's memory endure forever. The theme of *Lycidas* was far more intense and personal than anything else Milton had yet written. Most young adults seldom contemplate their own deaths—until one of their friends, someone their own age, dies. The premature death of one his Cambridge acquaintances made him acknowledge his own mortality. He could not help but apply Edward King's accident to his own circumstances. What if he too were to die before he achieved the fame and immortality for which he was working so hard? Milton's personal reaction to King's death added poignancy and power to the elegy he wrote.

But *Lycidas* has political as well as private themes. Religious revolt was spreading through England. In 1637, three Puritans—William Prynne, Henry Burton, and John Bastwick—had criticized the King's authority; they were punished by being sent to the pillory, where they lost their ears, followed by lifelong imprisonment. Their harsh sentence brought an outcry from the public, but the throne continued its strict stance throughout that year. In Scotland, an organized revolt was born, protesting the King's attempt to impose the Anglican Church's ritual on the Scottish church. This tide of bitter political feeling runs through *Lycidas*. As Milton mourned the loss of King's potential ministry, he condemned the Anglican Church's corrupt clergy.

Milton's mother died the same year he wrote *Lycidas*, and a few months later, Milton left England for the first time. At age 29, he set out to complete his education by traveling to France and Italy. His father generously financed his journey. Milton wanted to visit the famous Renaissance cities of Italy: Rome, Florence, and Naples. Although 17th century Italy was politically and economically oppressed, it was still considered to be a place of inspiration and pilgrimage, the center of Europe's artistic and intellectual life. Unfortunately, the Inquisition was in its power, and the Roman Catholic Church had a chokehold on the nation's intellectual life. Anyone who did not agree with the official opinions of the Roman Church was in danger of censorship or even more painful forms of persecution. Travelers to the country were advised to be discreet and keep their opinions to themselves. Before Milton had left on his journey, Sir Henry Wotton, once the ambassador to Venice, had passed this Italian proverb on to Milton as a word of advice: "Thoughts concealed and countenance open will go safely through the whole world."

In *Lycidas*, Milton had referred to the Roman Catholic Church as the "grim Wolf," but now he kept his disapproval to himself. He visited with a Cardinal in Rome and received a warm reception from a group of scholars in Florence. During his travels, Milton made many new friends and he composed several poems in Italian and Latin that brought him international fame. He even had an opportunity to speak with Galileo, the great astronomer.

Although Milton enjoyed his journey, he was disturbed by the intellectual climate he found in Italy. Later he wrote of his journey:

> I have sat among their learned men and been counted happy to be born in such a place of philosophic freedom as they supposed England was, while themselves did nothing but bemoan the servile condition into which learning amongst them was brought: that this it was which had damped the glory of Italian wits; that nothing had been there written now these many years but flattery and fustian. There it was that I found and visited the famous Galileo, grown old, a prisoner of the Inquisition for thinking of astronomy otherwise than the Franciscan and Dominican licensers thought.

Milton's travels gave him a new appreciation for his own nation. England had its problems, certainly, but at least the citizens had more intellectual and religious freedom than the Italians did.

Milton had planned to go on to Sicily and Athens, but while he was in Naples, he received sad news from home. His friend Charles Diodati had died. The political news was equally disturbing; war had broken out when Charles I attempted to impose Anglican bishops on the Presbyterian Church in Scotland. After fifteen months abroad, Milton now felt the need to return to England. In the summer of 1639, he went home. He found a nation in turmoil; the Scots had banded together to resist the King's religious authority.

When Charles led an army across the border into Scotland, his troops met with failure. The King then planned a second and stronger onslaught, and he called on Parliament to provide him with the money he needed for his massive military campaign. The House of Commons, however, refused to cooperate, and Charles I now found himself under attack from all sides. Parliament tried and executed the King's first minister, the Earl of Stafford, and sent the Archbishop of Canterbury, William Laud, to the Tower of London. Then Parliament went further and released the Puritan critics of the royal government that the King had imprisoned. Charles tried to reestablish his power with a military coup, but his plan failed. In 1642, as riots filled the streets of London and civil war broke out, Charles I fled.

Milton took lodgings in London where he would be close to the political action. He threw himself into the rebellion against the King's authority by writing pamphlets dealing with the Reformation and various aspects of church government. The language he used to condemn the bishops' power was aggressive. Events in London were becoming more violent. The conspirators in the Royalist coup were hanged in front of their own doors. Roman Catholic priests were hunted down and executed. Archbishop Laud, now a weak old man, was beheaded on Tower Hill. Meanwhile, the citizens of London suffered as they endured shortages of food and fuel caused by the war's restriction of trade. Many people, however, fiercely believed in Parliament's cause. Milton wrote that they hoped for "such a deliverance as shall never be forgotten by any revolution of time that this world hath to finish."

Milton had always believed he had a duty to use his talents and intellect for his country's service—but he also longed for peace so that he might pursue his own studies. He was now convinced that his life's work would be writing a great epic poem in English, and the political unrest postponed the day when he would be free to begin this work. "With what small willingness," he wrote, "I endure to ... leave a calm and pleasing solitariness fed with cheerful thoughts in a troubled sea of noises and harsh disputes." Instead of writing poetry, during these years most of Milton's effort went into the great flood of pamphlets that fluttered through London's streets.

Pamphleteering was a bustling business during England's Civil War. With the restrictions imposed by Charles I suddenly removed, the sense of freedom was heady. For the first time, printing presses were readily available, and people with strong opinions now had both the means and the freedom to spread their ideas to others. Men and women who had something to say published their thoughts for everyone to read. Theology and politics were the most common subjects, but people also wrote pamphlets on many other topics, from education to agriculture.
At first the pamphlets Milton wrote helped fuel the argument about church reform, but then he turned his attention to education. As noted earlier, *Of Education* was a call for more modern and creative methods in England's schools and universities. On a practical level, Milton expressed his interest in education by tutoring children, including his nephews, the two sons of his sister Ann. His instruction was imaginative, if somewhat demanding.

Personal and Political Troubles

In 1643, when Milton was thirty-four, he fell in love with a young girl from the country. Her father, a Royalist country squire, had borrowed money from Milton's father. Mary Powell was only seventeen, but she was beautiful and sweet, and Milton ignored the differences between them. He was so infatuated with her, that he married her after only a month's courtship.

The marriage was a disaster. Milton had expected his wife to share his intellectual interests, but Mary was unable to do so. She was bewildered by her new husband's expectations, and after a month she found an excuse to return to her family for a visit. Once there, she refused to return to London, using the war and her family's political position as an excuse.

Milton was deeply hurt and disappointed. He realized, however, that he was the one who had made a mistake. His misguided expectations and his haste to be married had led him into a union that was of no benefit to either partner. As he continued writing pamphlets to express his opinions, he turned now to a new topic: divorce. *The Doctrine and Discipline of Divorce* is full of his anger and bitterness, but it did point out a genuine societal problem. In the 17th century, social conventions forbade educated young men and women from courting before marriage. Once married, only the very rich and powerful saw divorce as an option, leaving the other ill-matched couples to muddle along as best they could. Recommending that divorce should be an option for everyone, as Milton did, was not an orthodox position to take in his day, especially from a person as religious and moral as Milton. However, he was not afraid of questioning the status quo, and his personal experience inspired him to be outspoken on this issue.

Parliament, however, was alarmed by the number of unconventional—and possibly dangerous—ideas that were springing into print. Some members of the House of Commons went so far as to recommend that censorship should be once more imposed. Suggestions like this worried Milton so much that he wrote and published a famous pamphlet, an appeal for freedom of the press that he called *Areopagitica*. (The Areopagus was the democratic assembly of ancient Athens.) In this pamphlet, Milton pled with Parliament to recognize that its own action had unleashed the free writing that now flourished in England. Did Parliament want to destroy the same liberty it had created by opposing the King? "Who kills a man kills a reasonable creature, God's image," Milton wrote; "but he who destroys a good book kills reason itself." Milton asserted that truth was never put to such a test: "Let her and Falsehood grapple," he wrote; "whoever knew Truth put to the worse in a free and open encounter?"

In the *Areopagitica*, Milton also expressed his faith in the new nation he was confidant would rise out of the Civil War.

> Methinks I see in my mind a noble and puissant nation rousing herself like a strong man after sleep and shaking her invincible locks. Methinks I see her like an eagle mewing her mighty young, and kindling her undazzled eyes at the full midday beam.

As the war continued, Milton's personal life was in difficult straits as well. When Cromwell, the House of Commons' Puritan leader, defeated the King in 1646, Milton's wife and her family were left in poverty and peril. Milton's friends arranged a meeting between him and his wife, who was now only a little more than 20. Her beauty and tears touched him, and he agreed to take her back. In fact, he felt so sorry for her that he also agreed to take in her entire family, despite their political differences.

His nephew, who was living with Milton at the time, described the couple's reunion as an "Act of Oblivion," which they agreed to on the past, combined with a "League of Peace," which they entered for the future. From then on their marriage seems to have been reasonably happy. They had two daughters together and a son who died as a baby.

Although Milton's personal life seemed to be stabilizing, the political atmosphere was rife with tension. He was deeply disappointed by political events. He was infuriated by the attempts of the Presbyterians in Parliament to limit religious freedom. In Milton's mind, religious freedom was one of the very causes that had justified the Civil War, and yet the Presbyterians now apparently believed that they were the only ones entitled to this liberty. He was even angrier when Parliament refused to pay the army that had won the war for their cause.

Charles I was not accepting his banishment quietly, and the nation's tense peace was short-lived. Charles' plots and schemes caused yet another civil war; when the army was again victorious against the king, it forcibly purged the House of Commons of all dissenters and took complete control of the nation. Under Oliver Cromwell's leadership, the army brought the King Charles I to trial.

Milton approved of these actions. In his opinion, God had brought justice to a corrupt ruler, who had betrayed his people. Milton went so far as to say that the King's death would make room for a more just and democratic government, which was referred to as a commonwealth. Others who shared his viewpoint were called "Commonwealthmen." Milton's ideas, however, were in some respects uniquely his own. They were based partly on the Bible, in which wicked kings were punished by divine retribution, and partly on what he knew about the Roman Republic from his classical studies.

During the cold winter of 1649, the King's trial held the attention of all England. A few days after the execution of Charles I, Milton, having put much thought into the matter, published a political pamphlet called The Tenure of Kings and Magistrates. In this work he argued that kings' power comes from their unspoken agreement with the people; this tacit contract makes kings the stewards of the commonwealth. When kings fail to carry out their responsibility—as Charles had failed—the people have the duty to call them to account. Milton's ideas were not new. The same philosophy had been used to justify the religious wars in France during the 16th century and the revolt of the Dutch against Phillip II of Spain.

The new government appreciated Milton's pamphlet because it helped counteract the tide of public opinion, which threatened to turn Charles I into a martyr. Throughout Charles's trial, and even when he mounted the scaffold, he had demonstrated a courageous dignity that had impressed all of England. After his death, a Royalist printer immediately released a little book of thoughts and prayers that the King was said to have composed during his captivity. The book was called *Eikon Basilike* (*The King's Image*), and it was instantly popular. Although the government tried to suppress the book, it was reprinted thirty-five times that same year. *Eikon Basilike* transformed Charles I into a Christian saint, who had bravely endured unjust persecution.

The leaders of the new Commonwealth of England turned to Milton for help. They asked him to compose a response to *Eikon Basilike*, refuting the image it portrayed of the King. Milton determined that he lacked the confidence to write anything powerful enough to undo the effects of the King's small book, but he was pleased to be asked. He believed wholeheartedly in the new government and he was glad to serve it in any way he could. However, his book, *Eikonoklastes* (*The Image Breaker*), was not his best writing. It had a petty, vindictive tone that tended to alienate readers rather than attract them to his point of view.

But the government had still more work for Milton. The exiled Royalists had asked one of the most famous European scholars to write a Latin work that defended Charles I, while it denounced the government that had been formed by his killers. The author, Salmasius, was internationally known, although his reputation and his work have not endured. The English Commonwealth, however, realized that Salmasius's book could have a powerful and detrimental effect on their government's reputation; the Commonwealth also recognized that Milton was the only English scholar with the required skill in Latin to refute the famous Salmasius. The government asked him to write an answer to Salmasius's work.

Milton responded with *Pro Populo Anglicano Defensio* (*In Defense of the English People*). The book attacked Salmasius personally, deflating his unjustified reputation; it also answered Salmasius's Royalist arguments point by point. *Defensio* was skillful and effective. Milton concluded it with a call to his fellow citizens to achieve still greater glories.

> After so glorious a deed, you ought to think, you ought to do nothing that is mean and petty, nothing but what is great and

sublime. To attain such praise there is only one way: as you have subdued your enemies in the field, so you shall prove that unarmed and surrounded by peace you of all mankind have the highest courage to subdue what conquers other nations—faction, avarice, the temptations of wealth and the corruptions that wait upon prosperity.

During the time of his professional triumph with *Defensio*, Milton's personal life was once more full of trials. His eyesight had been troubling him for years, and now, in the midst of the composition of *Defensio*, his vision failed him altogether. Though he had been having symptoms of vision deterioration for some time, he believed that his work on the book was responsible for his blindness; however, it was a sacrifice he gladly made for his country. Others, he wrote, had given their lives for the Commonwealth, while he had suffered a far lesser loss. Despite his brave resignation to his blindness, the loss of his sight was a terrible tragedy for Milton. He was a person who deeply enjoyed looking upon physical beauty and received so much satisfaction from reading and study. His blindness would make him intensely dependent on others.

A year after he went blind, another tragedy struck the Milton family. His wife Mary died shortly after giving birth to a third daughter leaving Milton with three young daughters to raise. Milton soon married again, but Katherine Woodhouse, his second wife, fell ill after giving birth to a daughter. She died on February 3, 1658, only fifteen months after their marriage. The daughter, also named Katherine, died the following month.

Milton honored his wife's death with a sonnet that began, "Methought I saw my late espoused saint...." The poem ended with these lines:

> Her face was veiled, yet to my fancied sight,
> Love, sweetness, goodness in her person shined
> So clear, as in no face with more delight.
> But O as to embrace me she inclined
> I waked, she fled, and day brought back my night.

The funeral Milton arranged for his wife indicated the depth of sorrow he felt at her death. The details of the funeral were expensive and elaborate, and Katherine was buried in a coffin with twelve locks. Milton gave the keys to these locks to twelve of his friends. What this symbolized to him is unclear, but the grief he felt after this brief marriage was seemed real and deep.

Meanwhile, despite his blindness, the Commonwealth continued to ask Milton for his service. Soon after the King's execution, the new government asked Milton to become Latin Secretary, which made him responsible for composing and proofreading all government correspondence with foreign powers. The Commonwealth knew that Royalists who had fled to other European nations were denouncing the new government's leaders as low-born illiterates. They were anxious to prove that the Royalists were wrong, and so they employed Milton's Latin skills in their service.

Two years later, in 1651, Milton was appointed Chief Censor. His job was to supervise the government's newspaper, *Mecurius Politicus*. In effect, however, he was asked to censor any book that did not support the government in which he believed. How could Milton, the author of the *Areopagitica*, reconcile this new job with his own ideals?

England was full of dissenting viewpoints. The Royalists continued their bitter attack against the new government, while the Presbyterians, who had wanted to reform the monarchy rather than destroy it all together, voiced their own criticisms. The Presbyterians had also hoped to make their church the national Church, and they were bitterly disappointed when Cromwell's government did not do so. Another group, the Levellers, hated the new government because they believed it had not gone far enough; led by the fanatic, John Lilburne, they wanted to completely reform the parliamentary system so that it would represent the interests of the common people, the artisans and yeomen who had never yet had a say in their government. Another extremist group, the Diggers, advocated the common ownership of land. All these groups expressed their beliefs vehemently in writing, and London's streets continued to be full of inflammatory pamphlets. Milton was incessantly busy keeping up with this huge tide of publications.

In addition there were the newspapers. The Dutch had only recently invented the newspaper in the 1620s, but the idea had spread quickly. In France, Cardinal Richelieu recognized that newspapers could be both dangerous and powerful, and he permitted only one government-controlled newspaper. King Charles I, however, had forbidden the publication of newspapers altogether. When his government collapsed, newspapers had sprung up almost overnight.

Most of them were merely small weekly pamphlets with eight to sixteen pages. Each issue contained a brief summary of the week's events with a short commentary from the editor. The editors (or printers) tried to make sure that each newspaper had a different publication day, so that Londoners could buy at least one new paper every day of the week. Some of these newspapers lasted only a few weeks before going out of business, but others continued to be printed for years. Many interest groups had their own newspapers, which functioned as their mouthpieces. The Levellers, for instance, published a newspaper called *The Moderate*.

Throughout the years of war, Parliament had occasionally suppressed a particular paper or arrested an editor. The Commonwealth Government decided to learn from Richelieu's example in France and make one newspaper its own. The government funded the paper, while it became an instrument for propaganda. The government's paper, the *Mercurius Politicus*, was edited by an intelligent and witty journalist named Marchamont Nedham. Nedham had been running a Parliamentary newspaper during the Civil War, but it had been bought by the King and for some months he had published an underground Royalist paper. Under the Commonwealth, Nedham returned to his earlier position. He and Milton became partners of a sort. Although they were very different from each other, Nedham was also a skilled writer, and he and Milton apparently worked well together. However, after a year, Milton was dismissed from his position as censor.

Milton was simply not suited for the job. He approved the publication in England of a book called *Racovian Catechism*, a work that denied the doctrine of the Trinity. When he was summoned to appear before the Council of State, he was asked why he would approve such a notoriously heretical work. He replied that he was only acting according to the same principles he had expressed in the *Areopagitica*. If the government did not like these principles, then Milton said he could no longer continue to be Chief Censor. The government agreed, and Milton no longer had any say over the nation's press. He did, however, maintain his job as Latin Secretary.

Milton was beginning to feel disillusioned with the Commonwealth. Like many others in England, he had hoped that the new government would be just and righteous. People idealistically referred to the Commonwealth as the "Rule of the Saints," and the events that followed the Commonwealth's birth encouraged people to think that, surely, God was on their side. Cromwell was able to quickly subdue both Ireland and Scotland, which had ultimately sided with the King. Then the Dutch, assuming that England would be exhausted by civil war, attacked by sea—and were completely defeated. Parliament had built enormous new ships, and the Puritan commanders—Robert Blake, Richard Deane, Edward Popham, and others—were brave and skillful seamen. Almost overnight, England became the ruler of the seas. For hopeful Englishmen like Milton, these events seemed to indicate that a new era of blessing and righteousness had dawned.

Unfortunately, the new government was in a state of chaos. Parliament failed to create a new national constitution, and it no longer represented the nation's citizens. In March 1653, Cromwell dissolved Parliament altogether and took the government into his own hands. He did, however, allow a new parliament to form that represented the Puritans' interests. This Puritan version of Parliament was mockingly referred to as "Barebone's Parliament." A prominent member of the ruling body was named Praisegod Barebone, and for many people in England, his name came to represent the Puritans' extreme and radical piety. The Puritans' Parliament intended to put into effect the Rule of the Saints, but its proposals were too extreme to be practical. In reality, the government was dependent on London's wealthy citizens for its finances; it could not simply dismiss these citizens' interests. Eventually, the idealistic group of men gave their authority back to Cromwell.

Oliver Cromwell took the title of Lord Protector. He believed that England should be ruled with the consent of Parliament, and he made an honest effort to rule accordingly. But England was simply too full of dissension; the many conflicting viewpoints could not reach consensus, and no manageable and truly representative Parliament could be called. Finally, Cromwell resorted to governing with the army's power. Even then, however, he did his best to govern within the structure of the English legal tradition as he understood it. His government was never a dictatorship and it was far more just than the government of many English kings.

History often looks back on this period of Puritan power as an austere and joyless era of English history. The Puritans did not approve of sinful and frivolous activities—like the theater—but during Cromwell's rule theatrical companies still performed in private homes. Chamber music was introduced as a form of entertainment at Cromwell's court, and something similar to a masque was performed at the marriage of his youngest daughter. He even granted a license to William Davenant to reopen the theater in Drury Lane, where the earliest operas in England were performed.

During Cromwell's rule, the first coffeehouses also opened in London. Meeting socially over a cup of coffee soon became the fashion, and the coffeehouses became meeting places for intellectual discussion of ideas and events. These establishments acted as informal clubs, but other, formal clubs grew out of this period as well. New ideas were springing up everywhere, and club members met to discuss the latest inventions and the most recent explorations in science. The most famous of these clubs met in Oxford, and is members included Robert Boyle and Christopher Wren. This group would later become the Royal Society, which still exists today.

Despite some of the freedoms that flourished under Cromwell's rule, Cromwell was hated by many. The Royalists looked on him as a king-murderer and a usurper. Some of his old friends and supporters hated him nearly as bitterly; they felt he had betrayed their hopes for an ideal government. Milton himself had been bitterly disillusioned during the years of political confusion. However, he continued to look to Cromwell as God's instrument of salvation for the nation. In Milton's mind, Cromwell was like the Old Testament Joshua, who had been chosen by God to do great things for his country.

In some ways, Cromwell lived up to Milton's ideals. After the English defeated the Dutch on the seas, Cromwell made peace and reformed the ancient English-Dutch alliance. He also stood up for a group of Protestants in the Italian Alps against whom the Duke of Savoy had launched a campaign to exterminate them. Milton was the one who wrote Cromwell's demand for international intervention to stop the Duke's evil violence. Milton was deeply moved by these actions. At the same time that he wrote Cromwell's letters, he wrote a sonnet containing these lines:

> Avenge O Lord thy slaughtered Saints, whose bones
> Lie scattered on the Alpine mountains cold....

Cromwell's active foreign policy kept Milton busy in his duties as Latin Secretary, since there were many diplomatic letters to be written to foreign leaders. Now that Milton was blind, he needed assistants in order to do his job; his principle helpers were his old friend Samuel

Hartlib, the poet Andrew Marvell, and eventually a young scholar named John Dryden, who would become a well-known writer in his own right.

On September 3, 1658, everything changed for Milton and his nation when Oliver Cromwell died. Immediately after Cromwell's death, the nation was preoccupied with mourning. His body was put on display for three weeks, and then it was replaced with a lifelike effigy. This majestic doll lay on a bed of state with a gold scepter in its right hand, the royal orb in its left, and a cap of purple velvet and ermine on its head. Eight silver candlesticks, five feet high, stood around the bed, and held three-foot candles that were kept constantly lit. The English people crowded to see their dead ruler. Ten weeks after his death, Cromwell was buried amid much pomp and ceremony.

Cromwell's son Richard was appointed in his place as Protector. However, Richard lacked his father's military genius, and the government began to crumble. Eventually, the army forced Richard to resign, and for more than a year the government was in chaos. The old Commonwealthmen fought with the army officers for power. In the end, the Scottish governor and general, George Monk, took advantage of the situation. He marched on London and declared the restoration of England's legitimate sovereign—Charles II. After twelve years of exile, Charles II was welcomed home by the English people, who were relieved to see an end of the turmoil. He would be one of England's most popular kings, and upon his return, London was full of rejoicing and celebration.

Milton, however, was full of despair. He watched with anguish as the same country that had fought for liberty now returned willingly to its old form of government. Desperate, he wrote another pamphlet, *The Ready and Easy Way to Establish a Free Commonwealth*, appealing to his fellow citizens to think twice before they returned to a monarchy. His words did not have the desired effect, however. His friends feared that his outspoken opinions would only get him into trouble with the newly restored king. They persuaded Milton to go into hiding. A friend, possibly a family member of his old comrade Charles Diodati, took him in.

Charles II, however, promised to forgive everyone whom Parliament did not decree exempt from pardon, but Milton had many Royalists enemies who tried hard to persuade the House of Commons that he be punished for his opinions. When Milton came out of hiding long enough to take a house in London for himself and his family, he was arrested and put into prison for about a month. Milton's old assistant, Andrew Marvell, was now a member of Parliament, and he spoke up for his old friend. The Royalist poet William Davenant joined Marvell in his plea on Milton's behalf. Eventually, even Milton's enemies were persuaded that God had already punished Milton enough by striking him blind. John Milton's name was included under the Act of Indemnity passed by Charles II, and Milton came out of hiding.

He may have been relieved to find that his life was not in danger after all, but nevertheless the year that followed was a trying one for Milton. The righteous government built on civil freedom was dead. Cromwell's body and the bodies of others who had served the Commonwealth were disinterred and hung from gallows for public display. Two of Milton's books, *Defense of the English People* against Salmasius and *Eikonklastes*, were censored, and all copies of the books that could be found were burnt. Many of Milton's colleagues and close friends were arrested and executed; some were beheaded while others were drawn and quartered.

Milton personally suffered great losses. He lost his position as Latin Secretary and all his savings, as well, since the Commonwealth's bank was dissolved when Charles II was restored to the throne. His job as secretary had included a house in London, the only place where he had lived since he went blind, and he was forced to leave this home.

The Inner Spirit

After all Milton had endured, his Muse, the powers of his imagination, had not forsaken him. He wrote:

> Standing on Earth, not rapt above the Pole;
> More safe I sing, with mortal voice unchang'd
> To hoarse or mute, though fall'n on evil days,
> On evil days though fall'n, and evil tongues;
> In darkness, and with dangers compassed round,
> And solitude; yet not alone, while thou
> Visit'st my slumbers nightly, or when Morn
> Purples the East: still govern thou my song,
> Urania, and fit audience find, though few.

When he was younger, he had planned to write an epic that was uniquely British, an Arthurian romance, but after all the political disillusionment he had experienced, Milton was no longer interested in Arthur and his knights. Instead, his imagination turned to something with a far greater scope—the Fall of Humanity, the beginning of sin.

Milton was blind when he began composing *Paradise Lost*. He had to dictate his words to an amanuensis and rely on his memory for the visual imagery he used. He was able to compose 40 or 50 lines of poetry in his head and hold them in his memory until he could dictate them. Then, he would make corrections when the lines were read back to him. As a result, the spoken quality of his words is an essential aspect of this poetry. He wrote poetry, which was intended to be *heard*.

Milton turned to the Bible for his source of inspiration. He had always believed that a poet's talents belonged to God; his own skill with words was an instrument to be used in God's service. After his painful disillusionment with England's government, Milton determined that a human paradise was not possible. He saw man's original Fall into sin as the point upon which human history turned. When Milton turned to the biblical account of Adam and Eve's surrender to temptation, he saw it as more than a story; it was also a statement about the nature of human beings: since the Fall, human beings were separated from God. However, the Church had traditionally interpreted the Bible story to also mean that the knowledge offered by the serpent to Adam and Eve was the corrupting element. In other words, too much knowledge leads to pride, which in turns leads to sin and death. Milton, however, could not accept this interpretation.

Milton firmly believed that knowledge and the ability to choose are *good*, not evil. In *Paradise Lost* he set out to create a concrete world to illustrate his spiritual beliefs. In doing so, he fleshed out the brief Bible story of Adam and Eve in a new way. He emphasized that it was not knowledge that brought about their downfall but disobedience to God. The Fall he described was the triumph of selfish passions over reason. In the same way that the English people had exercised their liberty by returning to political slavery under a monarchy, so Adam and Eve, according to Milton, used their powers of free choice to lose the bliss and security of Eden.

Milton presented the fall of the rebellious angels, as well. Some angels refused to accept man as a being worthy of paradise and rebelled against God's decision; as a result, God cast these angels from heaven into the doom of Hell. Much of *Paradise Lost* describes the perilous details of Hell. Some critics, including Johnson, the great 18th century man of letters, have complained that Milton's work has little to do with human affairs. But Milton was thoroughly disillusioned with human beings. At that point in his life, human actions had no meaning unless they were looked at in the light of heavenly affairs.

However, Milton's concept of heaven was no vague and hazy spiritual reality. Instead, Hell was described as a physical reality. Milton's God had a dark side; the God of *Paradise Lost* is self-righteous and cruel to his enemies. But the epic poem is also full of delight in both the created world and God's goodness. According to Milton, all the benefits of human life spring from God's love and creative mind. Ultimately, *Paradise Lost* was a statement of Milton's own faith in God. Even though Milton had endured much personal and public pain, he still believed that human life was an expression of divine meaning.

During the years that Milton worked on *Paradise Lost*, his personal life became more stable and contented. He was still dealing with the effects of his blindness, but servants and friends helped him compensate for the loss of his vision. Each morning, he would get up early, his mind already full of the next lines for his poem. By the time his amanuensis arrived, Milton would be ready to dictate. He also liked to have someone read to him from the Bible in Hebrew, and then he would eat a meager breakfast. After breakfast, he would spend the morning in study; he employed well-educated men who could read to him from Hebrew, Greek, Latin, Italian, Spanish, and French, as well as English. Later, in the day he would find a companion to go for a walk with him, leading him through the London streets. Whenever he could, Milton enjoyed meeting with his friends, and in the evening they would play and listen to music. Milton still had his father's old organ, and he moved it with him from residence to residence. He played it for his friends' pleasure.

Milton's three daughters, Anne, Mary, and Deborah, lived with him, but he was not close to the young girls. They had been raised mostly by their maternal grandmother and they had little sympathy for their father. They also had little interest in the books and learning that fascinated him so much. The rift between father and daughters was so great that Milton did not bother to tell the three girls when he married Elizabeth Minshull. When his middle daughter Mary heard the news from a servant, she said that it "was no news to hear of his wedding but if she could hear of his death that was something."

After his third marriage, Milton moved to a new house. His daughters took advantage of the chaos caused by moving to sell a large portion of their father's library. They also persuaded their servant to cheat their father out of housekeeping money. Milton's new wife had little patience with the three girls. She apprenticed Anne and Mary to gold-lacemakers, apparently to get the girls out of the house. However, she took good care of Milton, and his marriage seems to have been happy enough for the remainder of his life. Elizabeth, affectionately called "Betty," cooked his favorite dishes, and after dinner he would often accompany her on the organ while she sang. She also read to him in English from his favorite authors, Spenser, Shakespeare, and Crowley. Apparently, she had a good understanding of her husband and his work.

During these years, Milton became so famous that tourists, especially foreign ones, came by his house every day to catch a glimpse of the great author. One day the Duke of York, the brother of King Charles II and the future King James II, is said to have joined the sightseers outside Milton's door. Milton, used to turning away his uninvited visitors, invited him inside. As they talked, the Duke asked Milton if he believed that his blindness was God's judgment for what Milton had written against Charles I. Milton replied:

> If your Highness thinks that the calamities which befall us here are indications of the wrath of Heaven, in what manner are we to account for the fate of the King your father? The displeasure of Heaven, must, upon this supposition, have been much greater against him, than against me: for I have lost only my eyes, but he lost his head.

Milton's blindness probably tested his faith, but he held firm in his belief that God had inspired the Commonwealth that no longer existed. King Charles II, however, was a wise ruler who knew that revenge does little to promote a peaceful kingdom. He even went so far as to ask Milton to write for the Court, as Milton had once done for Cromwell. The poet replied that he could not "use his pen against his conscience."

In 1665, Milton's peaceful routine was disrupted when the plague struck London. The disease was carried by rats and communicated to humans by fleas, but in the 17th century, no one knew how the dread illness was spread. People burned fires on street corners, hoping the aromatic fumes would dispel the deadly air, and pedestrians buried their noses in pomanders as they walked through London's streets, believing that the sweet scent would help protect them. The plague had struck London many times since the 14th century, and during Milton's lifetime, 1625, 1636, and 1646 had all been bad plague years. But 1665 proved to be the worst year yet. At the peak of the epidemic, more than 2,000 people in London died each week; the total number of dead was about 60,000.

Those who could, left London, and friends persuaded Milton to do so as well. He and his family went to stay in a small cottage in Chalfont St. Giles, about twenty miles away from London. Milton, his wife, his three daughters, and their servant settled in the five-room house. The setting was not particularly conducive for spiritual thought and inspiration. Milton nevertheless rose at sunrise during the winter and at four in the morning during the summer months, so that he would have time to meditate upon his own life and the Bible. During Milton's time in Chalfont St. Giles, he may have resorted to asking his daughters to read to him, as he was isolated from his readers and amanuensis. Later, they recalled with bitterness being forced to read in foreign languages they did not understand.

No one knows for sure what he wrote during this time, but some historians speculate that during his time away from London, Milton wrote the play *Samson Agonistes*. Although the work was based on the biblical story of Samson, the Hebrew judge who ends his life blind and betrayed by his political enemies, it was in many ways Milton's spiritual autobiography. The work expresses Milton's own frustration, bitterness, and sorrow with lines such as:

> Why was my breeding ordered and prescribed
> As of a person separate to God,
> Designed for great exploits; if I must die
> Betrayed, captived, and both my eyes put out,
> Made of my enemies the scorn and gaze....
>
> Now blind, disheartened, shamed, dishonoured, quelled,
> To what can I be useful, wherein serve
> My nation, and the work from heaven imposed,
> But to sit idle on the household hearth,
> A burdenous drone; to visitants a gaze,
> Or pitied object....

However, *Samson* closes with a sense of triumph. Samson's "fiery virtue" is roused "from under ashes into sudden flame." For Milton, his own virtue was his poetry. Again, when the external events of his life looked their bleakest, his "Muse"—the divine grace of God's Spirit—continued to visit him with the creative power he expressed in his writing. At the end of *Samson*, Milton affirmed that inner and external peace and victory do not always run parallel.

When the plague abated, Milton was happy to return to London. However, he had not been back home long, when the Great Fire of London blazed through the city, turning two-thirds of it into ruins. Milton's own home was just outside the city walls and was untouched, but his old house on Bread Street, his old school, and the entire neighborhood around St. Paul's was destroyed. In his diary entry for September 2, 1666, a witness named John Evelyn described Londoners' hysteria during the fire:

> The conflagration was so universal, and the people so astonished, that from the beginning ... they hardly stirred to quench it, so as there was nothing heard or seen but crying out and lamentation, and running about like distracted creatures, without at all attempting to save even their goods; such a strange consternation there was upon them, so as it burned both in breadth and length, the churches, public halls, exchange, hospitals, monuments, and ornaments, leaping after a prodigious manner from house to house and street to street, at great distance from the other, for the heat (with a long set of fair and warm weather) had even ignited the air, and prepared the materials to conceive the fire, which devoured after an incredible manner, houses, furniture and everything.

Evelyn went on to describe "the noise and crackling thunder of the impetuous flames, the shrieking of women and children, the hurry of people, the fall of towers houses and churches ... like an hideous storm." The fire burned for days. When it was over, all that remained, according to Evelyn, was a "smoking and sultry heap which mounted up in dismal clouds night and day." Many wealthy people were reduced to poverty overnight.

Milton was fortunate to have escaped this disaster. (If he had not, the world would have forever lost *Paradise Lost* and *Samson Agonistes*.) However, he still owned the property on Bread Street, and the rent from this house had provided him with an income. Without it, he faced financial ruin. As a solution to his poverty, Milton began to look for a publisher for *Paradise Lost*. Most of the printing presses in London had been burned, but in April 1667, Samuel Simmons of Aldersgate Street gave him a down payment of five pounds for his epic. According to the contract Milton signed with Simmons, he would receive another five pounds when the first edition of 1300 copies had all been sold, and five pounds each if a second and third edition were also sold. For the 17th century, 1300 copies was a large edition, as the average print run for a pamphlet was only 500. To Milton's pleasure, the first edition sold through in two years. This would have meant that nearly every literate person in England at that time read *Paradise Lost*.

The court of Charles II loved bawdy and frivolous entertainment, but many English thinkers were preoccupied with more serious matters. The events of the previous years had made them think about mortality and the meaning of life. As a result, an intense interest in religion was thriving in England. John Bunyan, the uneducated Puritan, had begun writing his own fantastical religious prose, including *Pilgrim's Progress*, and the climate was receptive for Milton's great theological work.

For the first time, Milton became famous not simply as a man of learning, but as a poet. Some critics complained because the poem is written in blank verse, rather than the rhymed couplets that were popular at the time, but most people did not let this criticism disturb their admiration of the poem. Sir John Denham praised the work in the House of Commons, saying that it was "the noblest poem that ever was wrote in any language or any age." John Dryden, himself a master of the rhymed couplet, admitted, "This man cuts us all out, and the ancients too."

After all the sorrow and disillusionment of his life, Milton had at last accomplished the great goal he had aimed for since he was a young man—he had written a great work of English poetry. He would then turn his attention to another great work—*Paradise Regained*.

Paradise Regained

Paradise Regained is the story of the Incarnation of Christ. The Christ that Milton portrayed possessed a powerful intelligence and defeated all the arguments of Satan. In Milton's poem, Christ is unimpressed by earthly displays of power, whether that power be political or intellectual. For Milton, intellectual power clearly offered the greater temptation to pride and separation from God. He had always thought, however, that his life was dedicated to God, and he had spent much of his time reading the Bible. He read the Hebrew Old Testament every morning of his adult life, and the influence of these habits were clear in *Paradise Regained*.

In many ways, Milton was a Puritan in terms of theology. He believed that God's grace alone can redeem humanity, and he despised the authoritarian hierarchy of the Catholic Church. However, he also grew to have a deep respect for the Torah and the Jewish codes of behavior, and in this respect he was far different from most Puritans.

The Puritans' emphasis on the Old Testament, though, had led to a new interest in the Jewish faith in the 17th century. The Bishop of Exeter complained about the "jewism" in his diocese, and a group of extremists led by John Traske were imprisoned for practicing a form of Judaism. When they were released, they went to Amsterdam and joined a synagogue there.

Milton did not go this far, but his respect for Judaism had increased through his interactions with Jews. As Cromwell's Latin Secretary, Milton had negotiated with Rabbi Menasseh ben Israel for Jews to settle in London. Cromwell wanted the Jews in England partly because they brought with them trade that would enrich the nation's economy—and partly because he believed that the Bible prophesied that the Jews had to be dispersed throughout the earth before the world's redemption could begin. Menasseh ben Israel did come to London, on the condition that his people were allowed to worship God in their own way. A synagogue was built in London, and it was allowed to continue after the Restoration of Charles II. Many Londoners saw the synagogue services as a tourist attraction, but Milton would have appreciated the chance to hear the Hebrew he loved so much actually spoken and sung by native speakers.

In Milton's *Paradise Regained*, his Christ has an Old Testament quality. It is not Christ's death that mystically regains Paradise, as the Puritans believed; instead, Christ wins back Paradise by the way he lives his life—overcoming temptation through his self-discipline and qualities typically associated with great Hebrew kings, such as David. Although somewhat unorthodox, Milton's poem expresses his own faith in Christ. According to Milton, joy is the natural condition of God's creation. This joyful Paradise was lost when Adam and Eve disobeyed God—but it did not cease to exist. Instead, it was regained through Christ.

In Milton's personal life, he too had experienced this renewed sense of joy. He spent the last years of his life serenely. Betty and he lived alone in London; Anne and Mary were lacemakers, who lived independently from their father, and Deborah had gone to Ireland to be a lady's companion. Apparently, once she was away from home, Deborah thought more kindly of her father. Those who knew her remember her nostalgic recollections of her father's handsome face and his auburn hair (now streaked with gray) that she had so often combed and parted for him. When she had lived with him, they had quarreled often, but now she recalled his intelligent conversation and good-natured manners.

Yet the differences between father and daughters were never mended enough and they had no interest in receiving his books. As he grew older, Milton sold much of his library through his friend Millington, a bookseller who often walked with Milton through a nearby cemetery. During these years, Milton also sorted through his papers and manuscripts. He burned most of his personal letters, but he kept for posterity anything he thought might be useful for writing the Commonwealth's true history. He also sent some of his manuscripts to be published, including the *Brief History of Moscovia*, *The History of Britain*, and a volume that contained both *Samson Agonistes* and *Paradise Regained*. He also put together some other poems that had never before been published, and he issued a revised version of *Paradise Lost*. Milton had also presented his theological views in a long treatise titled *De Doctrina Christiana*. However, this work was too controversial for the 17th century, and despite his efforts, it was not published for another 140 years, when the more open-minded 18th century provided a more receptive climate for the text.

Many of the writers and thinkers of the 17th century, men who had once been close friends with Milton, were becoming more conservative as the years passed. As they did so, their friendships with Milton also cooled. They did not visit him as often, and occasionally they attacked his theology publicly. This rejection hurt and angered Milton, but the visitors he did have all remarked on his cheerfulness. He suffered from gout; his knuckles were swollen and he could no longer play the organ as easily as he once had. But according to one visitor, "he would be cheerful even in his gout-fits and sing."

When Charles II passed laws that favored Roman Catholic interests in England, Parliament insisted on repealing the laws. Milton responded with another pamphlet, this one called *Of True Religion, Heresy, Schism, Toleration, and what best means may be used against the growth of Popery*. In this little work, Milton said that all true religion was based on the Bible; he believed that the only heresy was "popery"—that is, when individuals rely on someone else to interpret God's revelation, rather than finding their own insights and inspiration. However, personally, Milton was tolerant of Roman Catholics. More and more of his friends, as well as his brother Christopher, were converting to Catholicism. Christopher, who was a London lawyer, visited his brother often. On July 20, 1674, when Christopher called on Milton, he found his brother ill. Milton told him he wished to make a will. According to Betty, Milton said to Christopher,

> Brother, the portion due to me from Mr Powell, my former wife's father, I leave to the unkind children I had by her; but I received no part of it, and my will and meaning is they shall have no other benefit of my estate than the said portion and what I have beside done for them. And all the residue of my estate I leave to the disposal of Elizabeth my loving wife.

By now, Milton was so crippled by arthritis and gout that he could no longer go for his walks around the cemetery with is friend Millington. Instead, he stayed at home. He nibbled at olives, which he had always liked, but ate very little else, and he enjoyed smoking, since it helped numb the pain in his hands. In November, his gout grew even worse. Surrounded by those who loved him, however, his life continued to be peaceful and cheerful. When he died, early in November of 1674, he went so quietly that those in the room did not at first notice he was dead. Had he lived another month, he would have been 66.

His funeral was a large one, and he was buried in the local cemetery. Later, in the 18th century, a group of drunken men exhumed his body and pulled the bones into pieces. The hair, teeth, fingers, ribs, and leg-bones were sold as relics. This final degradation seems eerily ironic for Milton, whose only solace seemed to rest in the belief that God would guard his eternal being until the moment of its awakening.

NEIL HEIMS

Milton: An Introduction

I

Milton's fame rests on the great poems of his last years, *Paradise Lost*, an epic retelling of the Old Testament story of the Fall, and *Paradise Regained*, a brief epic recounting Jesus' victory over Satan. For the modern reader, these are difficult poems in which unfamiliar English runs on in long sentences about Adam and Eve, God, Jesus, the Devil, sin, and disobedience. Milton has been stereotyped as ponderous and not overly exciting. Legend has it that in the nineteenth century children were made to memorize lines of Milton as punishment. But Milton's poetry is worth deep examination. Not only is it ornately baroque and brilliantly crafted, but it is the poetry of a man intellectually and practically involved with the daily problems of liberty and authority, with matters which have marked the exercise of citizenship in the years since the French and American revolutions. Much of his labor, in fact, was spent putting aside poetry, and writing political and ecclesiastical pamphlets defending liberty of conscience and parliamentary government. Milton opposed the bishops (or prelates) of the church and the king of England, argued for freedom of the press and the right of the people to change their government, and saw his hope for reform vanish when the Commonwealth he was part of fell and monarchy was restored.

The problem which taxed Milton and especially informs his last works is reconciling God's goodness and Mankind's evil. Milton believed in political and ecclesiastical liberty. He also saw a revolution fail and a great deal of human corruption. How a person can still believe in the right of liberty, and how one can hope that people will exercise liberty rightly are the main concerns of his writing. *Paradise Lost* is his response. Liberty is always at risk. God, Milton argues made man "sufficient to stand but free to fall." Satan, thereafter, in his humiliated pride at not being God, stands always ready to corrupt God's creatures. Liberty, thus, is not only possible; it is inherent, but it is under continuous threat of being lost should a person fall for the satanic vision which perceives disobedience as liberty. People must understand freedom and be knowledgeable decision makers in order to be able to resist temptations to sin. To be so armed people must be well educated, able to reason, and aware that reasoning is of limited value for choosing virtuously if it is not guided by devotion to God.

The vision of liberty presented in Milton's poetry and prose is tempered by, and founded on, a profound Puritan faith in divine providence, in Christ, and the innate human capacity for reasoning, and choosing the good. Milton's craft—the structure of his prose syntax, the shape of his blank verse paragraphs, the way he drew the meaning of the words he used—devolved from his prodigious learning. He was fluent in five languages besides his native English: Greek, Latin, Hebrew, French, and Italian. He was steeped in classical, biblical, medieval and Renaissance literature and philosophy. He was a musician, and played the organ, and he was current on the scientific discoveries and theories of his own era. Milton's father was an educated and well-to-do man, a scrivener by trade, and respected as a musician. Some of his works were published in a volume, which also contained pieces by the great Elizabethan composer, William Byrd. He could afford to give Milton a comfortable environment in which to develop his gift for the humanities, especially poetry. As a young man, Milton hoped to prepare for the clergy, but chose to be a poet, and his poetry frequently reflects his life-long concern with improving the human lot in a fallen world of sin and suffering through devotion to the eternal, transcendent God and obedience to his law. As a poet, too, he was the guardian of European humanism, and the trumpet of God's rectitude. *Paradise Lost*, accordingly, presents the story of the creation and the fall of man from the Book of Genesis within the formal structure of the epic as developed by Homer and Virgil. *Samson Agonistes* presents biblical material, the story of Samson from the Book of Judges, in the form of a Greek tragedy. Milton's complexity comes from his desire to craft his poetry out of all the cultural materials at his disposal, to reflect God's eternal time as well as the experience of his own time. His poetry was the result of his engagement with both the secular and the divine. He did not distinguish between them, just as he saw no contradiction between liberty as a man and obedience as a creature of God.

For Milton, religion was not an isolated or otherworldly practice, despite the fact that a reader of his verse might imagine him perfectly content to sing God's glory. This very disposition forced him into politics and polemics, as if his basic complaint were that the conditions of civil monarchy and prelatic rule in the Church got in the way of each person's ability to express devotion to God. Milton did not object to bowing before majesty, when it was the majesty of God. The king and the bishops, as Milton saw it, usurped God's place in the Church; they had to be removed.

II

Because Milton was equally concerned with the craft of poetry and expounding Christian doctrine, Protestant freedom of conscience and political liberty, critical examination of his poetry has been divided, sometimes focusing on one aspect or the other, sometimes bringing the two together. Dr. Johnson, in his *Life of Milton* condemns *Lycidas*, the pastoral elegy Milton wrote in 1637 mourning the drowning of a fellow Cambridge student, Edward King, as bad poetry. He writes, "…the diction is harsh, the rhymes uncertain, and the numbers unpleasing." He doubts the authenticity of *Lycidas*' sentiments or its passion, and complains that it is lacking in unity as well as nature, truth, and art; and that "whatever images it can supply, are long ago exhausted."[1] However, by the middle of the twentieth century, *Lycidas* had come to have "sovereign status among English elegies and within English poetry in general."[2] Critics see it as giving voice to some of the on-going concerns of Milton's career, the corruption of the clergy, his ambition to write a great poem, his place inside literary tradition, and Christ's defeat of sin and death. Admiration does not indicate, however, that elements which troubled Dr. Johnson and others have been resolved. Rather than being dismissed as a failure, the poem is appreciated for its complexity and mysteries, which proper understanding can unravel to reveal a depth of truth that poetry plays at concealing. Elements perceived as faults—its pastoral artificiality or apparent lack of coherence—have become the focus of scholarship and interpretation.

Much critical thought about Milton, however, focuses on the content of his poetry. William Empson, for example, condemns Milton's "downright horrible conception of God," but not his poetry. He sees the poetry at odds with the doctrine, and argues that despite the doctrine, Milton "yet keep[s] somehow alive, underneath it, all the breadth and generosity, the welcome to every noble pleasure, which had been prominent in European history just before his time."[3]

Perhaps nowhere is an ambivalent attitude toward Milton better to be observed than in T.S. Eliot's famous pair of essays, the 1936 condemnation of Milton's person, his achievement and his influence, and Eliot's apparent recantation delivered in 1947. Eliot is equally put off by the craft and the content. He begins in 1936 by admitting that Milton is "a very great poet indeed," but immediately adds that "it is something of a puzzle to decide in what his greatness consists," offering this catalogue of his faults: "Either from the moralist's point of view, or from the theologian's point of view, or from the psychologist's point of view, or from that of the political philosopher, or judging by the ordinary standards of likeableness in human beings, Milton is unsatisfactory."[4] One need not look far, if so inclined, for ammunition to support this harsh indictment. Dr. Johnson is a rich source. On successive pages he condemns Milton for peevishness and hypocrisy (McAdam, 363), for being frugal in the praise of others (366), for having an offensive character (372), and for using indecent language in his defense of regicide (375). Empson, as we have just seen, called Milton's concept of God "horrible." In 1944, Robert Graves published *Wife to Mr. Milton*, a historical novel written from the point of view of Marie Powell, Milton's first wife, depicting the poet as a proud, impatient, self-esteeming man, choleric when crossed, pedantic, tediously disputatious, and ill-disposed to consider the sensibilities of others.[5]

Eliot's chief objection to Milton, despite his stinging characterization, rests on his verse, which, although idiosyncratic, he says, is so powerful that it stymied the ability of subsequent poets to write good verse. He admits that their weakness ought not to be blamed on Milton; but, beyond Milton's baleful influence, the quality of the verse itself disturbs Eliot. Milton's poetry, according to Eliot, suffers from a "withered sensuousness." He attributes it to Milton's "early book-learning," and says it was reinforced by his blindness. In consequence, Eliot argues, Milton's poetry lacks the kind of "visual imagination" so richly apparent in Shakespeare. Overcompensating for a weakness in picturing, Eliot says Milton places too great an emphasis on the sound of the poetry in order to convey sensation, sometimes at the expense of meaning. Milton's syntax, Eliot asserts, is not determined by thought or idea, but by "the musical significance, by the auditory imagination" (Eliot, 157-161). F.R. Leavis makes a similar point when he complains of Milton's "concern for mellifluousness—for liquid sentences and a pleasing opening and closing of vowels," which generates words with "no pressure behind" them.[6]

These observations imply that in Milton's work we derive impressions of the events of the poet's imagination more from the sound of his words and how they echo than we do from a sharp image or from precise statements. Eliot suggests that even Milton's Grand Style, constructed of long and Latinate periodic sentences, often of a wandering complexity, and composed of words stripped to their root meanings is the natural outcome of a visual impairment. The surge of the music energizes the movement of the serpentine verse, carrying verse and reader along, even if bits of meaning are left behind. In his 1947 reconsideration, Eliot argues that imprecision is appropriate to Milton's subject because that subject is, in *Paradise Lost*, set in a world which does not materially exist.[7] Eliot seems to imply that Milton leads readers into acquiescing rather than reasoning them into agreement or convincing them by true images.

One only needs to look at Christopher Ricks' dazzling study of how Milton uses sound to draw depth of meaning from the word "heart" in *Paradise Lost*[8] to see that Eliot is, of course, right in saying that sound is very important to Milton. However, if meaning and doctrine, story and lesson are conveyed in ways which by-pass the rational faculties, through the hypnotic seduction of sound and syntax, or by sophistry, the poem is violating its own credo. Milton's major theme, after all, is the importance of informed, conscientious, and free choice. But the poem does not violate its own credo. Milton's greatness resides, in part, in his ability to convey content through the combined aural, visual, and intellectual powers of his verse. With the help of a few examples, let us see how this works.

John Hollander points us to Milton's own commentary on the effects of music and what kind of meaning music conveys.[9] Referring to lines 552-557 in Book II of *Paradise Lost*:

> Thir song was partial, but the harmony
> (What could it less when Spirits immortal sing?)
> Suspended Hell, and took with ravishment
> The thronging audience. In discourse more sweet
> (For Eloquence the Soul, Song charms the Sense,)
> Others apart sat on a Hill retir'd,

Hollander writes:

> No matter what the perverse import of the text of the devils' epic song, the melody itself, partaking of the potency of the heavenly music, remains strongly effective. The notions of word and note are separated in Hell; it is the doctrine which has suffered in the fall of the rebel angels, rather than the purely musical power to charm and move. But Milton carefully stipulates that it is the soul itself that is affected by the "rational" powers of "Eloquence," while "Song charms the Sense" alone and cannot, no matter how attractive, actually operate upon the highest psychic faculties. (317)

Hollander emphasizes that the passage indicates Milton's awareness of the uncanny and untrustworthy charm of music, and of sensuousness itself.

The characteristic syntactic complexity in this passage represents a style of Milton's verse Eliot calls "tortuous" (159). Actually, this sort of verse provides an example of the mimetic function of sound popular in seventeenth century music. In Handel's *Messiah*, for example, the music shakes as the singer sings, "And I will shake all nations," or flattens out when he sings the phrase, "the crooked straight and the rough places plain." In Haydn's oratorio, *The Creation*—a setting in German translation of verses from the Bible and from *Paradise Lost*—when the chorus sings the word "*licht*," "light" in "Let there be light," the previously hushed singing blazes.

The syntax of Milton's verse, as in the lines just cited concerning the fallen angels' recreations does not replace or obscure meaning, but contributes to it. Here the meaning of the sentence is suspended between the words, "harmony" and "suspended," for a full line by the parenthetical question. The syntax not only imitates the sense of the verse—thought, like the operation of Hell, is suspended for a beat—but is an ingredient in the depiction of the state of the fallen angels and replicates their condition. Their moment of recreation suspends the eternal quality of their torment, but, in a moment, that suspension will be removed and torment resumed. Complicated syntax is not a barrier to meaning. Instead, such syntax reinforces the idea that the reader must pay attention, (just as we must be alert to sin) and read analytically against the flow of the music, (just as we must be able to resist the flood of disobedient appetite) or slip on the verse and lose footing (or fall, through transgression, and lose paradise).

Milton's verse (and also his prose) uses sound to support both imagery and syntax. The three combine to produce the sensuousness of music, the recognition of sight, and the rationality of intellect, in a context that activates the force of judgment. As an example, let us look at the following passage:

> Him the Almighty Power
> Hurl'd headlong flaming from th' Ethereal Sky
> With hideous ruin and combustion down
> To bottomless perdition, there to dwell
> In Adamantine Chains, and Penal Fire
> Who durst defy the Omnipotent to Arms. (P.L. I.44-49)

This verse is dramatic, didactic, visual and kinetic. The intricacy of the syntax and the broad arc of melody enhance these qualities. The first word "*Him*" (being the objective) points at Satan, as if in a warning,— watch out for *him!*—but also shows Satan's mistaken view of his own centrality as the object of God's concern and as his own chief object. It signals that Satan is not the *subject* of the poem, despite his prominence. "*Him* the Almighty Power/ Hurl'd" (emphasis added). Sound, syntax, and imagery contribute to each other, and together produce meaning. Line by line the syntax and the sound shift focus to fit the imagery. The language moves perception from Satan's sense of himself to the casting out—the onomatopoeic "Hurl'd." Then comes the free fall, "headlong flaming from the "Ethereal Sky," then the motion and the result, "down," then the false finality of "there to dwell," because the torment of loss does not achieve closure. The enjambment of the verse suggests the *ongoing* suffering: "In Adamantine Chains and penal Fire." The passage, not the devil, comes to rest with the reading of the charges, "Who durst defy th'Omnipotent to arms."

As important as sound is for Milton, an examination of a more purely visual passage can show us that Milton also paints clearly and quietly with words:

> Under a tuft of shade that on a green
> Stood whispering soft, by a fresh fountain side
> They sat them down, and after no more toil
> ...grateful, to their Supper Fruits they fell,
> Nectarine Fruits which the compliant boughs
> Yielded them, side-long as they sat recline
> On the soft downy Bank damaskt with flow'rs:
> The savory pulp they chew, and in the rind
> Still as they thirsted scoop the brimming stream;
> ...About them frisking play'd
> All Beasts of th'Earth...
> Sporting the Lion ramp'd, and in his paw
> Dandl'd the Kid; Bears, Tigers, Ounces, Pards
> Gamboll'd before them, th'unwieldy Elephant
> To make them mirth us'd all his might, and wreath'd
> His lithe Proboscis...(P.L., IV, 325-347)

In his 1947 essay, Eliot remarked that "[w]e must ... in reading *Paradise Lost*, not expect to see clearly, our sense of sight must be blurred" (178). These lines present an idealized picture of paradise. The poignancy of these lines is not a result of their music, but a result of the contrast between the picture of the young lovers content in a landscape, which reflects their blissfulness and our knowledge that it is to be short-lived because of the Fiend.

Despite Eliot's assertion that the Grand Style encourages and benefits from diffuse imagery, Milton's epic use of imagery is clear, focused, and dramatic. In characteristic epic similes, meanings are embedded in tableaux. Here is one of Milton's, again from Book IV of *Paradise Lost*. Through Satan's eyes we first see the garden and Adam and Eve. Along with Satan, we have seen them happy in their unfallen state, unaware they are in his sight. A troop of heavenly angels led by Gabriel, sent to the garden to find and expel Satan, surprise him at night at their side as they sleep, "Squat like a Toad, close to the ear of *Eve*/ Assaying by his Devilish art to reach/ The Organs of her Fancy" (*P.L.* IV, 800-803). When the angel Ithuriel "with his Spear/ Touch'd" Satan in his toad form "lightly,...up he starts/ Discover'd and surpris'd." Milton uses an epic simile to describe the metamorphosis:

> ...As when a spark
> Lights on a heap of nitrous Powder, laid
> Fit for the Tun some Magazin to store
> Against a rumor'd War, the Smutty grain
> With sudden blaze diffus'd, inflames the Air:
> So started up in his own shape the Fiend. (*P.L.* IV, 814-819)

Satan explodes into himself like gunpowder at a spark's touch. The simile not only *represents* the event by a sensational image; the visual violence of that image also *characterizes* Satan's nature and the threat he poses. By associating gunpowder with Satan, Milton alludes to his introduction of what was in the seventeenth century a modern and anti-chivalric technology. Additionally, the image judges him; he is smutty with the flames of hell around him. The word "lights," although it reminds us of "light," is stripped of that meaning. It is used as a synonym for "settles," and suggests that the only light coming from Satan is a flash which consumes, not a "bright effluence." It suggests the instantaneous explosion of our paradise when Satan settles on us.

Milton's use of language is so controlled that he can create an image through sound. In the first seven lines of Book IX of *Paradise Lost*, for example, the words "discourse," "distrust," "disloyal," "distance," "distaste," and "disespous'd" appear. What they have in common is the hissing prefix "dis," reminiscent of the sibilance of a snake, the persona Satan assumes as he sets about deceiving Eve. "Dis" also is one of the Latin names for the Roman god of the underworld. Milton uses it in relation to Satan in Book IV of *Paradise Lost* when describing the landscape of paradise as fairest of all landscapes, including

> ...that fair field
> Of Enna, where Proserpin gath'ring flow'res
> Herself a fairer Flow'r by gloomy *Dis*
> Was gather'd, which cost *Ceres* all that pain....(P.L. IV,268-271)

Using words prefixed by "dis," Milton sets the figure of Satan hovering over the beginning of the book in which he will accomplish later his dreaded goal of the Fall, and associates him with negation. Without the apparent use of imagery, Milton has fixed the image of Satan in the reader's mind.

Milton's ability to transform abstract ideas and values into imagery gives Milton's poetry—not just *Paradise Lost* and *Paradise Regained*, but *Comus*, *The Nativity Ode*, and *Samson Agonistes*, too—dramatic reality, and provides a metaphysical space with what appears to be substantiality. The image of light, for instance, in *Paradise Lost* not only signifies clarity and goodness or acts metaphorically to symbolize an attribute of God and indicate the phenomenon through which he manifests himself. God *is* light, actually. Here is the introduction to Book III:

> Hail holy Light, offspring of heaven's first born
> Or of th'Eternal Coeternal beam
> May I express thee unblam'd? since God is Light,
> And never but in unapproached Light
> Dwelt from Eternity, dwelt in thee,
> Bright effluence of bright essence increate. (III. 1-6)

Because Milton is formulating a concept as well as concretizing the phenomenology of an invisible world, divinity and light are represented by an image which is as intellectual and abstract as it is sensuous: "Bright effluence of bright essence increate." The image is intended to convey a suggestion of the flooding substance of an invisible God into whose presence the reader is about to be introduced. It is a light inside the mind. At the same time, he is invoking this representational power of light, Milton is also referring to the light which we all (but not the blind poet) see every day. With the third book, the action of the poem is moving out of the (metaphorical and literal) dark realms of Hell into the upper realms where there is daylight.

III

The substance and apparent intention of Milton's poetry are probably as troublesome to the average modern reader as the density, complexity, and erudition of his verse. Having abandoned early plans to be a clergyman in order to pursue poetry, Milton nevertheless, retained the desire to minister to fallen mankind, and to instruct us in the ways of

God and godliness. The poetry is devotional, an offering to God designed to instruct us in God's ways and our responsibilities. Milton's method, Stanley Fish argues, involves entangling the reader in the characters' errors in relation to God and God's will in order to accomplish the reader's humiliation and, thereby, the reader's education.[10] Milton is concerned with values, behavior, and belief (ours), and wants to influence both them and us. C. S. Lewis, who favors the kind of Christian reading Empson abhors argues that

> [*Paradise Lost*] is a poem depicting the objective pattern of things, the attempted destruction of that pattern by rebellious self love, and the triumphant absorption of that rebellion into a yet more complete pattern. The cosmic story—the ultimate *plot* in which all other stories are episodes—is set before us. We are invited, for the time being, to look at it from outside. And that is not, in itself, a religious exercise. *When we remember that we also have our places in this plot*, that we also, at any given moment are moving either towards the Messianic or towards the Satanic position, *then we are entering the world of religion*....(last sentence emphasis added.)[11]

Fish makes specific what Lewis leaves to implication. We don't chance to "remember that we also have our place in this plot;" Milton repeatedly reminds us of it.

> ...the reader is drawn into the poem, not as an observer who coolly notes the interaction of patterns..., but as a participant whose mind is the *locus* of that interaction. Milton insists on this since his concern with the reader is necessarily more direct than it might be in any other poem; and to grant the reader the status of the slightly arrogant perceiver-of-ironies...would be to deny him the full *benefit* (I use the word deliberately, confident that Milton would approve) of the reading experience. (Fish, 11-12)

In Sonnet XIX, "On His Blindness," a poem in which Milton worries that he is not using his talent as he ought to, he states directly that his role as a poet is "to serve [his] Maker," now, in this world. In

Paradise Lost, he says the primary task of that service is to "assert Eternal Providence/ And justify the ways of God to men." His duty to God is to show that the responsibility for the woeful state of the fallen world is mankind's, not God's.

Milton uses evil figures like Satan, Comus or Dalila to prod representatives of mankind—like Adam and Eve, the Lady in *Comus*, Jesus in his human incarnation in *Paradise Regained*, and Samson—to stray from virtue, from obedience to God, and from their proper calling. They are deceivers who seduce in order to enslave. The drama and the didacticism of Milton's poetry emerge from the protagonists' struggles to achieve and maintain strength and determination against enslaving seductions. It is hot midday, in *Paradise Lost*, Eve is hungry, and the alluring apple must not be bitten. Samson, embodying as he does the struggle between blinding passion and clear duty in *Samson Agonistes*, makes a perfect hero for Milton. Milton's villains present evil as enticing and glamorous. They endow it with the allure of what we know we ought not to want and need someone else to draw us to attempt. Milton exposes the glamour as deceptive, and unworthy of our interest. He insists that we possess the power to resist evil and scorn temptation, and he glorifies the spheres where evil does not govern, flooding them with joyful radiance. The apparent sweetness of evil Milton illustrates throughout his work is only the foretaste of bitterness, the liberty of doing evil, the prelude to a damnable and humiliating bondage. His sermon is that, with clarity of mind founded on good precepts and a devotion to godly obedience, evil can be resisted. Milton's 1634 *Mask performed at Ludlow Castle*, usually called *Comus*, presented before the Earl of Bridgewater in his honor, is one of his early essays in the discipline of scorning temptation.

In the masque two brothers and their sister, undertake a perilous journey to their father's house through a dark wood haunted by a dangerous enchanter. The three children are the Earl's actual children, and the conclusion of the masque presents these children safely to their actual father. The masque with its symbolic plot is an allegory for teaching virtue, an educational exercise for the children, and a gift to the Earl. In the course of the journey, the sister is separated from her brothers and taken prisoner by Comus, the enchanter who haunts the woods, waylaying travelers and turning them into bestial revelers. The Lady resists his advances, arguing that he can "not touch the freedom of my mind/ With all [his] charms," although he has immobilized her body.

Debonairly Comus responds with suave reasoning which he hopes will confuse her as he offers her a flaming "cordial Julep" which will transform her into one of his bestial rout. She retorts,

> *Lady.* 'Twill not restore the truth and honesty
> That thou hast banish't from thy tongue with lies....
> I would not taste thy treasonous offer: none
> But such as are good men can give good things,
> And that which is not good, is not delicious
> To a well-govern'd and wise appetite. (*Comus*, 690-705)

This is a model of the Miltonic encounter between good and evil and a central theme for Milton. Evil gains entrance through a vulnerable appetite. When Eve meets Satan in the ninth book of *Paradise Lost*, she does "taste [the] treasonous offer." When Satan appeals to Jesus in the wilderness (in the second book of *Paradise Regained*, beginning at line 368) to "sit down and eat," Jesus rebuffs him saying, "And with my hunger what hast thou to do?" When Samson is blind and bound in Gaza, and his treacherous wife Dalila offers to intercede with the Philistine leaders to take him home and give him solace and nursing, he cries, "No, no, of my condition take no care" (928). At the heart of the encounter is the argument that we are responsible if we succumb to evil because virtue can transcend appetite and resist evil through the combined power of reasoning and a vision of the good.

Because Milton portrays the devil and his surrogates with a complex and human character, which he probes with psychological brilliance, giving the devil great poetry, some serious readers have asserted that Milton's sympathies, despite his overt allegiance to Christian doctrine, are with the devil. Blake, for example, has famously written that "The reason Milton wrote in fetters when he wrote of Angels & God and at liberty when of Devils & Hell, is because he was a true Poet and of the Devil's party without knowing it."[12] Shelley in his *Defense of Poetry* similarly sees Satan as a heroic figure:

> Nothing can exceed the energy and magnificence of the character of Satan as expressed in *Paradise Lost*. It is a mistake to suppose that he could ever have been intended for the popular personification of evil.... Milton's Devil as a moral being is as far superior to his God, as one who

> perseveres in some purpose which he has conceived to be excellent in spite of adversity and torture is to one who in the cold security of undoubted triumph inflicts horrible revenge upon his enemy, not from any mistaken notion of inducing him to repent of a perseverance in enmity, but with the alleged design of exasperating him to deserve new torments. Milton has so far violated the popular creed ... as to have alleged no superiority of moral virtue to his God over his Devil.[13]

C. S. Lewis contradicts this view with a character analysis of Satan-in-his-context and a homily, concluding that:

> to admire Satan ... is to give one's vote not only to a world of misery, but also for a world of lies and propaganda, of wishful thinking, of incessant autobiography. Yet the choice is possible. Hardly a day passes without some slight movement towards it in each of us. That is what makes *Paradise Lost* so serious a poem. The thing is possible, and the exposure of it is resented (102-3).

Irene Samuel defends the theological validity and the dramatic integrity of Milton's conception and presentation of God. Writing of God's first appearance in Book III of *Paradise Lost*, she says:

> ...as soon as we take Milton's God as Being, infinitely beyond all created beings, the scene has dramatic point. The near tonelessness of his first speech at once proves itself the right tone. It has offended readers because they assume that the "I" who speaks is or should be a person like other persons. The flat statement of fact, past, present, and future, the calm analysis and judgment of deeds and principles—these naturally strike the ear that has heard Satan's ringing utterances as cold and impersonal. They should. For the omniscient voice of the omnipotent moral law speaks simply what is. Here is no orator using rhetoric to persuade, but the nature of things expounding itself in order to present fact and principle unadorned.

Clearly Milton uses that toneless voice of the moral law to destroy immediately the straw figure of a gloating, tyrannical victor that Satan and his followers had conjured up in Books I and II.[14]

Even from this brief survey it is clear that Milton's work engenders conflicting opinions and may be seen to be weighing conflicting values. This is fitting for the time in which Milton lived, when institutional dogma and authority were being challenged by inner light, individualism, and conscience, when absolutism was being forced to yield to argument and parliament, and when observation and reason were held to have greater authority than obedience and assertion. His engagement with his time and its religious and political conflicts, combined with his solid faith not only in God, but in *his* vision of God and the absolutism of Good, are at the root of his work.

IV

Even in a corrupt England when the hope and promise of revolution have failed, or in *Samson Agonistes* when the Philistines have overthrown the God of Israel and Samson himself has betrayed his own strength and duty, Milton has a strong faith that the abilities to reason and to choose are the powers which define being human. They are inherent, inalienable constituents of our being, which we can cultivate or thwart. They constitute our weapons in the struggle against Satan because knowing good and evil, Milton believes, enables us to refuse evil. This power is determined by the human ability to give dimension to a spiritual and invisible world, more real because more enduring, than the phenomenological world of our senses. It is a platonic concept Milton was particularly equipped to express and explore because of his blindness. He himself writes that the failure of his mortal sight strengthened his vision of immortal forms:

> Seasons return, but not to me returns
> Day, or the sweet approach of Ev'n or Morn,
> Or sight of vernal bloom, or Summer's Rose,
> Or flocks, or herds, or human face divine;
> But cloud instead, and ever-during dark

> Surrounds me, from the cheerful ways of men
> Cut off, and for the Book of knowledge fair
> Presented with a Universal blanc
> Of Nature's works to me expung'd and rais'd,
> And wisdom at one entrance quite shut out.
> So much the rather thou Celestial Light
> Shine inward, and the mind through all her powers
> Irradiate, there plant eyes, all mist from thence
> Purge and disperse, that I may see and tell
> Of things invisible to mortal sight. (P.L. III, 41-55)

The vision of the immortal and invisible, of the celestial light which shines inward, is a stronger and truer vision than the vision afforded to or by the mortal eyes, as lovely and desirable as Milton writes it may be. Satan exploits our attachment to this mortal vision, and his success lies in his ability to supplant the truth of the immortal vision in our consciousness with the false allure of the mortal one. The only real power that mankind possesses, in Milton's view, is the power to apprehend the immortal vision, for it places the reality of God's eternity over the temporality of earthly suffering. This is a familiar position, both Christian and Platonic, which can be used to justify either one of two contradictory attitudes. The vision of the invisible world can release one from concern about the visible world, or, as in Milton's case, it can provide the image of the standard people must adhere to as they confront the fallen world. In either case, material reality reflects our relation to since it is a result of our relation to the ideal.

This faculty which results from being able to reason and to choose between good and evil, and thereby to participate in creating the way of the world, is freedom. Although freedom, Milton believes, is an inherent constituent of being human, it can be either a strength or a weakness. It makes humanity capable of sin as well as obedience. Education is of such great importance to Milton because, by developing our capacity to know, it determines our ability to choose between sin and obedience. In 1644, in *Of Education*, Milton wrote "[t]he end ... of learning is to repair the ruins of our first parents by regaining to know God aright, and ... by possessing our souls of true virtue...."[15] After "...years and good general precepts," the curriculum he designs "will have furnished [his pupils] more distinctly with that act of reason which in ethics is called Proairesis." ("Proairesis" is the word Aristotle uses in the *Nicomachean*

Ethics, II. iv, 3, to signify the act of choosing between good and evil.) Milton outlines a rigorous curriculum which includes along with the studies of Classical and Biblical authors, the Italian language, economics, "the beginning, end, and reasons of political societies,...the grounds of law and legal justice, ... all the Roman edicts and tables with their Justinian, and so down to the Saxon and common laws of England, and the statutes." Lastly, Milton prescribes logic, rhetoric, and poetry, the disciplines essential to fashioning our capacity to choose and defend liberty and rectitude (635-6). Arthur Barker drew the connection between learning and virtue for Milton this way:

> [He] was never the helpless and passive recipient of divine assistance; such support came to him from the studious summoning up of "all his reason and deliberation." The voices which heartened him employed no mystical utterance; they spoke in the phrases of divine philosophy and with the ordered rhythms of classical poetry. The light which broke forth, God-given though it was, was never blindingly mysterious; it was that intellectual ray, the candle of the Lord.[16]

Milton dramatizes the importance of learning and knowing in Book VIII of *Paradise Lost* when the archangel Raphael visits Adam and Eve in Paradise. Come to warn them about Satan, he must give them a full account of the nature, history and politics of heaven and earth. He provides not only information, but philosophy, too, telling them how to think and what disposition to cultivate. Discussing astronomy, for example, Raphael presents the alternative heliocentric and geocentric theories, teaching Adam and Eve the formulation "What if ... this?" and "What if ... the other?"(Book VIII, l.122) as well as teaching them conflicting theories of motion. And then he tells them not to concern themselves with which is "right," but to be "lowly wise." Knowledge of the phenomenological world is subject to interpretation and pragmatic, of the invisible world it is absolute. The very indeterminacy of knowledge of the physical world, Raphael indicates, is a theological design. Because heaven, for example, is distant we can know that we cannot know everything there is to know, everything that God knows. The very knowledge of the limitation of human knowledge and understanding which Raphael imparts is part of the education of mankind and strengthens the ability to choose between good and evil.

For Milton, knowledge is always, at its root, knowledge of good and evil; this knowledge is essential because it enables us to stand, and makes falling our own choice. Liberty of choice governs all of Milton's work whether in the realm of religion, politics, or marriage and divorce. It is his faith that the capacity for liberty of choice defines humanity and cannot exist if we are ignorant. This theme and its centrality appear in a well known cluster of images in the speech he made to the Parliament of England in 1644 for the defense of unlicensed printing, the *Areopagitica*:

> Good and evil we know in the field of this world grow up together almost inseparably; and the knowledge of good is so involved and interwoven with the knowledge of evil, and in so many cunning resemblances hardly to be discerned, that those confused seeds which were imposed on Psyche as an incessant labor to cull out and sort asunder, were not more intermixed. It was from out the rind of one apple tasted that knowledge of good and evil, as two twins cleaving together, leaped forth into the world. And perhaps this is that doom which Adam fell into of knowing good and evil, that is to say, of knowing good by evil. (Hughes, 728)

Good and evil define each other, and we define ourselves by choosing between them. It is the same lesson Milton teaches in the concluding scenes of *Paradise Regained*. Jesus needs the Satanic temptations in order to be defined as the Savior. The Satanic evil is a necessary element in the Christian good. The "doom" Milton speaks of in *Areopagitica* is not only a punishment, but a fate. The nature of being (which Irene Samuel calls Milton's God) determines that we must choose. Not only must we be free in order to choose, but because we cannot do anything but choose, we *are*, like it or not, free. Despite apparent metaphysical differences, the distance between Milton and Sartre when it comes to defining the human burden is not very great.

Crippling our capacity to choose does not destroy the need or the obligation to choose; it reduces us. The essential Miltonic paradox is that his doctrine of liberty is in the service of duty. Milton's argument for liberty—of printing, of marriage, of conscience—is an argument for establishing an environment which allows us to perform our duty. The forbidden tree in the Garden of Eden is an emblem of the interconnection of freedom and duty. Without the ability and the opportunity to choose, people are not free. Adam tells Eve:

> ...God left free the Will, for what obeys
> Reason, is free, and Reason he made right,
> But bid her well beware, and still erect,
> Lest by some fair appearing good surpris'd
> She dictate false, and misinform the Will
> To do what God expressly hath forbid. (P.L., IX, 351-356)

Reason guides choice, but reason can reason wrongly if it is without reference to knowledge and a vision of the good, if it is uneducated and uninstructed. Accidental goodness, goodness stumbled upon rather than chosen, being "dumbly good" is not showing goodness at all because it lacks the elements of awareness and deliberateness, which reflect the will of the person. Milton makes this plain in another famous section of *Areopagitica*:

> I cannot praise a fugitive and cloistered virtue, unexercised and unbreathed, that never sallies out and sees her adversary, but slinks out of the race where that immortal garland is to be run for, not without dust and heat. Assuredly we bring not innocence into the world, we bring impurity much rather: that which purifies us is trial, and trial is by what is contrary. That virtue therefore which is but a youngling in contemplation of evil, and knows not the utmost that vice promises to her followers, and rejects it, is but a blank virtue, not a pure; ...therefore, the knowledge and survey of vice is in this world ... necessary to the constituting of human virtue, and the scanning of error to the confirmation of truth....
> (Hughes, 728)

The forbidden tree in the pre-lapsarian world, not evil in itself, but affording the opportunity for transgression, represents a central symbol of Milton's philosophy. It stands as something whose existence in the garden turns the abstract doctrine of radical choice into a concrete necessity and a continuous possibility. Before our first parents ate from the forbidden tree, their knowledge of good and evil was distant and abstract. It was a disease in the environment. After eating, they knew evil experientially, having been infected by it. They knew good by its sudden absence. Milton's concept of knowing, for all his book learning, is inextricably bound to doing.

The knowledge of good and evil is not contained in a thing but revealed in a process. The *act* of biting the apple, the enactment of disobedience, is what indicates a choice to step out of God's realm into the Devil's, just as the act of drinking the Julep in *Comus* is, more than the julep itself, the danger the Lady faces. They symbolize the act of participating in evil. And although Adam and Eve's transgression symbolizes the archetypal choosing of sin, Milton also presents it as an archetypal lesson from which we may learn, and which can strengthen our ability to resist transgression.

The activity of choosing is paramount. Without the opportunity for disobedience, obedience would not be the sign of freely given devotion to God. Satan would then be right in his accusation that God is a tyrant. Our virtue and devotion to God would only be a form of programmed circuitry, and there would be no mechanism for freedom. This is what God is saying in Book III of *Paradise Lost*.

> ... I have made him just and right,
> Sufficient to have stood, though free to fall.
> Such I created all th'Ethereal Powers
> And Spirits, both them who stood and them who fail'd;
> Freely they stood who stood, and fell who fell.
> Not free, what proof could they have giv'n sincere
> Of true allegiance, constant Faith and Love,
> Where only what they needs must do, appear'd?
> Not what they would? What praise could they receive?
> What pleasure I from such obedience paid,
> When Will and Reason (Reason also is choice)
> Useless and vain, of freedom both despoil'd,
> Made passive both, had serv'd necessity,
> Not mee. (P.L. III, 98-111)

Milton believes in the power of the individual conscience—the authority of "th' upright heart and pure" (*P.L.* I. 19)—and the importance of individual choice. Human virtue is only authentic when freely chosen, authorized by reason as well as faith, and not the result of being bound to the discipline of authority despite Milton's emphasis on obedience. God's assertion of man's freedom is especially important because the Protestantism to which Milton adhered gives credence to the doctrine of Predestination. Milton must show this freedom as an actual human possibility rather than a cruel Divine perversity. Milton defines Predestination as God's foreknowledge of what man will do, but not, Milton insists, God's foreordination of that behavior. Predestination is not a function of God's control over each person but of the differing relation God and Mankind have to time. For God, all time is always present; for his human creatures time unravels in the finitude of the temporal sequence we are limited to perceiving. While God sees and knows the outcome of the free play of the creatures he made free, he has not made the outcome. For Milton, God has left to us some of the power of creation. Although we may neither see nor know the outcome of our endeavors, it does not mean we are not devising it. That is the painful truth of tragedy. For Milton, the free exercise of Christian virtue, informed by a vision of the eternal invisible world, which he has depicted in his work, is its antidote.

Notes

1. McAdam, E. L. Jr. and George Milne, eds. *"Life of Milton."* In *A Johnson Reader*, New York: The Modern Library, 1966, p. 406.

2. Lawry, Jon S. "'Eager Thought': Dialectic in Lycidas." In *PMLA*, LXXVII (1962), 27.

3. Empson, William. *"Milton's God.* Cambridge: Cambridge University Press (1961), 276-277.

4. Eliot, T. S. "Milton I." In *On Poetry and Poets*. New York: Farrar, Straus and Cudahy (1957), 156.

5. Graves, Robert. Wife to Mr. Milton. New York: Creative Age Press, Inc. (1944), 380 p.

6. Leavis, F. R. *Revaluation: Tradition and Development in English Poetry*. New York, W.W. Norton (1963).

7. Eliot, T. S. "Milton II." In *On Poetry and Poets*. New York: Farrar, Straus and Cudahy (1957), 178.

8. See Ricks, Christopher. "John Milton: Sound and Sense in *Paradise Lost.*" In *The Force of Poetry*. Oxford: Oxford University Press (1987), 60-79.

9. Hollander, John. "Milton's Renewed Song." In *The Untuning of the Sky*. Princeton: Princeton University Press (1961), 315-331.

10. Fish, Stanley Eugene. *Surprised by Sin: the Reader in Paradise Lost*. Berkeley: The University of California Press (1971), xiii.

11. Lewis, C. S. *A Preface to* Paradise Lost. London: Oxford University Press (1974), 132.

12. Blake, William. *The Poetry and Prose of William Blake*. Edited by David V. Erdman. Commentary by Harold Bloom. Garden City, NY: Doubleday & Company (1970), 36.

13. Shelley, Percy Bysshe. "A Defense of Poetry." In *The Selected Poetry and Prose of Percy Bysshe Shelley*. Edited, with an Introduction by Carlos Baker. New York: The Modern Library College Editions, 512.

14. Samuel, Irene. "The Dialogue in Heaven: A Reconsideration of *Paradise Lost*, III, 1-417. *PMLA* (1957).

15. Milton, John. "Of Education." In *John Milton: Complete Poems and Major Prose*. Edited by Merritt Y. Hughes. New York: The Odyssey Press (1957), 631.

16. Barker, Arthur. "The Voice of Reason." In *Milton and the Puritan Dilemma*. Toronto: the University of Toronto Press (1942), 81.

T. S. ELIOT

On Poetry and Poets

MILTON I*

While it must be admitted that Milton is a very great poet indeed, it is something of a puzzle to decide in what his greatness consists. On analysis, the marks against him appear both more numerous and more significant than the marks to his credit. As a man, he is antipathetic. Either from the moralist's point of view, or from the theologian's point of view, or from the psychologist's point of view, or from that of the political philosopher, or judging by the ordinary standards of likeableness in human beings, Milton is unsatisfactory. The doubts which I have to express about him are more serious than these. His greatness as a poet has been sufficiently celebrated, though I think largely for the wrong reasons, and without the proper reservations. His misdeeds as a poet have been called attention to, as by Mr. Ezra Pound, but usually in passing. What seems to me necessary is to assert at the same time his greatness—in that what he could do well he did better than anyone else has ever done—and the serious charges to be made against him, in respect of the deterioration—the peculiar kind of deterioration—to which he subjected the language.

"Milton I" and "Milton II" from *On Poetry and Poets* by T.S. Eliot. Copyright © 1957 by T.S. Eliot. Copyright renewed © 1985 by Valerie Eliot. Reprinted by permission of Farrar, Straus and Giroux, LLC.

* Contributed to *Essays and Studies of The English Association*, Oxford University Press, 1936.

57

Many people will agree that a man may be a great artist, and yet have a bad influence. There is more of Milton's influence in the badness of the bad verse of the eighteenth century than of anybody's else: he certainly did more harm than Dryden and Pope, and perhaps a good deal of the obloquy which has fallen on these two poets, especially the latter, because of their influence, ought to be transferred to Milton. But to put the matter simply in terms of 'bad influence' is not necessarily to bring a serious charge: because a good deal of the responsibility, when we state the problem in these terms, may devolve on the eighteenth-century poets themselves for being such bad poets that they were incapable of being influenced except for ill. There is a good deal more to the charge against Milton than this; and it appears a good deal more serious if we affirm that Milton's poetry could only be an influence for the worse, upon any poet whatever. It is more serious, also, if we affirm that Milton's bad influence may be traced much farther than the eighteenth century, and much farther than upon bad poets: if we say that it was an influence against which we still have to struggle.

There is a large class of persons, including some who appear in print as critics, who regard any censure upon a 'great' poet as a breach of the peace, as an act of wanton iconoclasm, or even hoodlumism. The kind of derogatory criticism that I have to make upon Milton is not intended for such persons, who cannot understand that it is more important, in some vital respects, to be a *good* poet than to be a *great* poet; and of what I have to say I consider that the only jury of judgment is that of the ablest poetical practitioners of my own time.

The most important fact about Milton, for my purpose, is his blindness. I do not mean that to go blind in middle life is itself enough to determine the whole nature of a man's poetry. Blindness must be considered in conjunction with Milton's personality and character, and the peculiar education which he received. It must also be considered in connexion with his devotion to, and expertness in, the art of music. Had Milton been a man of very keen senses—I mean of *all* the five senses—his blindness would not have mattered so much. But for a man whose sensuousness, such as it was, had been withered early by book-learning, and whose gifts were naturally aural, it mattered a great deal. It would seem, indeed, to have helped him to concentrate on what he could do best.

At no period is the visual imagination conspicuous in Milton's poetry. It would be as well to have a few illustrations of what I mean by visual imagination. From *Macbeth*:

> This guest of summer,
> The temple-haunting martlet, does approve
> By his loved mansionry that the heaven's breath
> Smells wooingly here: no jutty, frieze,
> Buttress, nor coign of vantage, but this bird
> Hath made his pendent bed and procreant cradle:
> Where they most breed and haunt, I have observed
> The air is delicate.

It may be observed that such an image, as well as another familiar quotation from a little later in the same play,

> Light thickens, and the crow
> Makes wing to the rocky wood

not only offer something to the eye, but, so to speak, to the common sense. I mean that they convey the feeling of being in a particular place at a particular time. The comparison with Shakespeare offers another indication of the peculiarity of Milton. With Shakespeare, far more than with any other poet in English, the combinations of words offer perpetual novelty; they enlarge the meaning of the individual words joined: thus 'procreant cradle', 'rooky wood.' In comparison, Milton's images do not give this sense of particularity, nor are the separate words developed in significance. His language is, if one may use the term without disparagement, *artificial* and *conventional*.

> O'er the smooth enamel'd green ...

> ... paths of this drear wood
> The nodding horror of whose shady brows
> Threats the forlorn and wandering passenger.

['Shady brow' here is a diminution of the value of the two words from their use in the line from *Dr. Faustus*.

> Shadowing more beauty in their airy brows.]

The imagery in *L'Allegro* and *Il Penseroso* is all general:

> While the ploughman near at hand,
> Whistles o'er the furrowed land,
> And the milkmaid singeth blithe,
> And the mower whets his scythe,
> And every shepherd tells his tale,
> Under the hawthorn in the dale.

It is not a particular ploughman, milkmaid, and shepherd that Milton sees [as Wordsworth might see them]; the sensuous effect of these verses is entirely on the ear, and is joined to the concepts of ploughman, milkmaid, and shepherd. Even in his most mature work, Milton does not infuse new life into the word, as Shakespeare does.

> The sun to me is dark
> And silent as the moon,
> When she deserts the night
> Hid in her vacant interlunar cave.

Here *interlunar* is certainly a stroke of genius, but is merely combined with 'vacant' and 'cave', rather than giving and receiving life from them. Thus it is not so unfair, as it might at first appear, to say that Milton writes English like a dead language. The criticism has been made with regard to his involved syntax. But a tortuous style, when its peculiarity is aimed at precision [as with Henry James], is not necessarily a dead one; only when the complication is dictated by a demand of verbal music, instead of by any demand of sense.

> Thrones, dominations, princedoms, virtues, powers,
> If these magnific titles yet remain
> Not merely titular, since by decree
> Another now hath to himself engrossed
> All power, and us eclipsed under the name
> Of King anointed, for whom all this haste
> Of midnight march, and hurried meeting here,
> This only to consult how we may best
> With what may be devised of honours new
> Receive him coming to receive from us
> Knee-tribute yet unpaid, prostration vile,
> Too much to one, but double how endured,
> To one and to his image now proclaimed?

With which compare:

'However, he didn't mind thinking that if Cissy should prove all that was likely enough their having a subject in common couldn't but practically conduce; though the moral of it all amounted rather to a portent, the one that Haughty, by the same token, had done least to reassure him against, of the extent to which the native jungle harboured the female specimen and to which its ostensible cover, the vast level of mixed growths stirred wavingly in whatever breeze, was apt to be identifiable but as an agitation of the latest redundant thing in ladies' hats.'

This quotation, taken almost at random from *The Ivory Tower*, is not intended to represent Henry James at any hypothetical 'best', any more than the noble passage from *Paradise Lost* is meant to be Milton's hypothetical worst. The question is the difference of intention, in the elaboration of styles both of which depart so far from lucid simplicity. The sound, of course, is never irrelevant, and the style of James certainly depends for its effect a good deal on the sound of a voice, James's own, painfully explaining. But the complication, with James, is due to a determination not to simplify, and in that simplification lose any of the real intricacies and by-paths of mental movement; whereas the complication of a Miltonic sentence is an active complication, a complication deliberately introduced into what was a previously simplified and abstract thought. The dark angel here is not *thinking* or conversing, but making a speech carefully prepared for him; and the arrangement is for the sake of musical value, not for significance. A straightforward utterance, as of a Homeric or Dantesque character, would make the speaker very much more real to us; but reality is no part of the intention. We have in fact to read such a passage not analytically, to get the poetic impression. I am not suggesting that Milton has no idea to convey which he regards as important: only that the syntax is determined by the musical significance, by the auditory imagination, rather than by the attempt to follow actual speech or thought. It is at least more nearly possible to distinguish the pleasure which arises from the *noise*, from the pleasure due to other elements, than with the verse of Shakespeare, in which the auditory imagination and the imagination of the other senses are more nearly fused, and fused together with the thought. The result with Milton is, in one sense of the word, *rhetoric*. That term is not intended to be derogatory. This kind of 'rhetoric' is not necessarily bad in its influence; but it may be considered bad in relation to the historical life of a language as a whole. I have said elsewhere that the living English which was Shakespeare's became split up into two components one of which was exploited by Milton and the other by Dryden. Of the two, I still think Dryden's development the healthier, because it was Dryden who preserved, so far as it was preserved at all, the tradition of conversational language in poetry: and I might add that it seems to me easier to get back to healthy language from Dryden than it is to get back to it from Milton. For what such a generalization is worth, Milton's influence on the eighteenth century was much more deplorable than Dryden's.

If several very important reservations and exceptions are made, I think that it is not unprofitable to compare Milton's development with that of James Joyce. The initial similarities are musical taste and abilities, followed by musical training, wide and curious knowledge, gift for acquiring languages, and remarkable powers of memory perhaps fortified by defective vision. The important difference is that Joyce's imagination is not naturally of so purely auditory a type as Milton's. In his early work, and at least in part of *Ulysses*, there is visual and other imagination of the highest kind; and I may be mistaken in thinking that the later part of *Ulysses* shows a turning from the visible world to draw rather on the resources of phantasmagoria. In any case, one may suppose that the replenishment of visual imagery during later years has been insufficient; so that what I find in *Work in Progress* is an auditory imagination abnormally sharpened at the expense of the visual. There is still a little to be seen, and what there is to see is worth looking at. And I would repeat that with Joyce this development seems to me largely due to circumstances: whereas Milton may be said never to have seen anything. For Milton, therefore, the concentration on sound was wholly a benefit. Indeed, I find, in reading *Paradise Lost*, that I am happiest where there is least to visualize. The eye is not shocked in his twilit Hell as it is in the Garden of Eden, where I for one can get pleasure from the verse only by the deliberate effort not to visualize Adam and Eve and their surroundings.

I am not suggesting any close parallel between the 'rhetoric' of Milton and the later style of Joyce. It is a different music; and Joyce always maintains some contact with the conversational tone. But it may prove to be equally a blind alley for the future development of the language.

A disadvantage of the rhetorical style appears to be, that a dislocation takes place, through the hypertrophy of the auditory imagination at the expense of the visual and tactile, so that the inner meaning is separated from the surface, and tends to become something occult, or at least without effect upon the reader until fully understood. To extract everything possible from *Paradise Lost*, it would seem necessary to read it in two different ways, first solely for the sound, and second for the sense. The full beauty of his long periods can hardly be enjoyed while we are wrestling with the meaning as well; and for the pleasure of the ear the meaning is hardly necessary, except in so far as certain key-words indicate the emotional tone of the passage. Now Shakespeare, or Dante, will bear innumerable readings, but at each reading all the elements of appreciation can be present. There is no interruption between the surface that these poets present to you and the core. While therefore, I cannot pretend to have penetrated to any 'secret' of these poets, I feel that such appreciation of their work as I am capable of points in the right direction; whereas I cannot feel that my appreciation of Milton leads anywhere outside of the mazes of sound. That, I feel, would be the matter for a separate study, like that of Blake's prophetic books; it might be well worth the trouble, but would have little to do with my interest in the poetry. So far as I perceive anything, it is a glimpse of a theology that I find in large part repellent, expressed through a mythology which would have better been left in the Book of *Genesis*, upon which Milton has not improved. There seems to me to be a division, in Milton, between the philosopher or theologian and the poet; and, for the latter, I suspect also that this concentration upon the auditory imagination leads to at least an occasional levity. I can enjoy the roll of

> ... Cambula, seat of Cathaian Can
> And Samarchand by Oxus, Temir's throne,
> To Paquin of Sinaean kings, and thence
> To Agra and Lahor of great Mogul
> Down to the golden Chersonese, or where
> The Persian in Ecbatan sate, or since
> In Hispahan, or where the Russian Ksar
> On Mosco, or the Sultan in Bizance,
> Turchestan-born ...,

and the rest of it, but I feel that this is not serious poetry, not poetry fully occupied about its business, but rather a solemn game. More often, admittedly, Milton uses proper names in moderation, to obtain the same effect of magnificence with them as does Marlowe—nowhere perhaps better than in the passage from *Lycidas*:

> Whether beyond the stormy Hebrides,
> Where thou perhaps under the whelming tide
> Visit'st the bottom of the monstrous world;
> Or whether thou to our moist vows deny'd
> Sleep'st by the fable of Bellerus old,
> Where the great vision of the guarded Mount
> Looks toward Namancos and Bayona's hold.

than which for the single effect of grandeur of sound, there is nothing finer in poetry.

I make no attempt to appraise the 'greatness' of Milton in relation to poets who seem to me more comprehensive and better balanced; it has seemed to me more fruitful for the present to press the parallel between *Paradise Lost* and *Work in Progress*; and both Milton and Joyce are so exalted in their own kinds, in the whole of literature, that the only writers with whom to compare them are writers who have attempted something very different. Our views about Joyce, in any case, must remain at the present time tentative. But there are two attitudes both of which are necessary and right to adopt in considering the work of any poet. One is when we isolate him, when we try to understand the rules of his own game, adopt his own point of view: the other, perhaps less usual, is when we measure him by outside standards, most pertinently by the standards of language and of something called Poetry, in our own language and in the whole history of European literature. It is from the second point of view that my objections to Milton are made: it is from this point of view that we can go so far as to say that, although his work realizes superbly one important element in poetry, he may still be considered as having done damage to the English language from which it has not wholly recovered.

Milton II*

Samuel Johnson, addressing himself to examine Milton's versification, in the *Rambler* of Saturday, January 12, 1751, thought it necessary to excuse his temerity in writing upon a subject already so fully discussed. In justification of his essay this great critic and poet remarked: 'There are, in every age, new errors to be rectified, and new prejudices to be opposed.' I am obliged to phrase my own apology rather differently. The errors of our own times have been rectified by vigorous hands, and the prejudices opposed by commanding voices. Some of the errors and prejudices have been associated with my own name, and of these in particular I shall find myself impelled to speak; it will, I hope, be attributed to me for modesty rather than for conceit if I maintain that no one can correct an error with better authority than the person who has been held responsible for it. And there is, I think, another justification for my speaking about Milton, besides the singular one which I have just given. The champions of Milton in our time, with one notable exception, have been scholars and teachers. I have no claim to be either: I am aware that my only claim upon your attention, in speaking of Milton or of any other great poet, is by appeal to your curiosity, in the hope that you may care to know what a contemporary writer of verse thinks of one of his predecessors.

I believe that the scholar and the practitioner in the field of literary criticism should supplement each other's work. The criticism of the practitioner will be all the better, certainly, if he is not wholly destitute of scholarship; and the criticism of the scholar will be all the better if he has some experience of the difficulties of writing verse. But the orientation of the two critics is different. The scholar is more concerned with the understanding of the masterpiece in the environment of its author: with the world in which that author lived, the temper of his age, his intellectual formation, the books which he had read, and the influences which had moulded him. The practitioner is concerned less with the author than with the poem; and with the poem in relation to his own age. He asks: Of what *use* is the poetry of this poet to poets writing to-day? Is it, or can it become, a living force in English poetry still

---

*The Henrietta Hertz Lecture, delivered to the British Academy, 1947, and subsequently at the Frick Museum, New York.

unwritten? So we may say that the scholar's interest is in the permanent, the practitioner's in the immediate. The scholar can teach us where we should bestow our *admiration* and *respect*: the practitioner should be able, when he is the right poet talking about the right poet, to make an old masterpiece actual, give it contemporary importance, and persuade his audience that it is interesting, exciting, enjoyable, and *active*. I can give only one example of contemporary criticism of Milton, by a critic of the type to which I belong if I have any critical pretensions at all: that is the Introduction to Milton's *English Poems* in the 'World Classics' series, by the late Charles Williams. It is not a comprehensive essay; it is notable primarily because it provides the best prolegomenon to *Comus* which any modern reader could have; but what distinguishes it throughout [and the same is true of most of Williams's critical writing] is the author's warmth of feeling and his success in communicating it to the reader. In this, so far as I am aware, the essay of Williams is a solitary example.

I think it is useful, in such an examination as I propose to make, to keep in mind some critic of the past, of one's own type, by whom to measure one's opinions: a critic sufficiently remote in time, for his local errors and prejudices to be not identical with one's own. That is why I began by quoting Samuel Johnson. It will hardly be contested that as a critic of poetry Johnson wrote as a practitioner and not as a scholar. Because he was a poet himself, and a good poet, what he wrote about poetry must be read with respect. And unless we know and appreciate Johnson's poetry we cannot judge either the merits or the limitations of his criticism. It is a pity that what the common reader to-day has read, or has remembered, or has seen quoted, are mostly those few statements of Johnson's from which later critics have vehemently dissented. But when Johnson held an opinion which seems to us wrong, we are never safe in dismissing it without inquiring why he was wrong; he had his own 'errors and prejudices', certainly, but for lack of examining them sympathetically we are always in danger of merely countering error with error and prejudice with prejudice. Now Johnson was, in his day, very much a modern: he was concerned with how poetry should be written in his own time. The fact that he came towards the end, rather than the beginning of a style, the fact that his time was rapidly passing away, and that the canons of taste which he observed were about to fall into desuetude, does not diminish the interest of his criticism. Nor does the likelihood that the development of poetry in the next fifty years will take quite different directions from those which to me seem desirable to explore, deter me from asking the questions that Johnson implied: How should poetry be written now? and what place does the answer to this question give to Milton? And I think that the answers to these questions may be different now from the answers that were correct twenty-five years ago.

There is one prejudice against Milton, apparent on almost every page of Johnson's *Life of Milton*, which I imagine is still general: we, however, with a longer historical perspective, are in a better position than was Johnson to recognize it and to make allowance for it. This is a prejudice which I share myself: an antipathy towards Milton the man. Of this in itself I have nothing further to say: all that is necessary is to record one's awareness of it. But this prejudice is often involved with another, more obscure: and I do not think that Johnson had disengaged the two in his own mind. The fact is simply that the Civil War of the seventeenth century, in which Milton is a symbolic figure, has never been concluded. The Civil War is not ended: I question whether any serious civil war ever does end. Throughout that period English society was so convulsed and divided that the effects are still felt. Reading Johnson's essay one is always aware that Johnson was obstinately and passionately of another party. No other English poet, not Wordsworth, or Shelley, lived through or took sides in such momentous events as did Milton; of no other poet is it so difficult to consider the poetry simply as poetry, without our theological and political dispositions, conscious and unconscious, inherited or acquired, making an unlawful entry. And the danger is all the greater because these emotions now take different vestures. It is now considered grotesque, on political grounds, to be of the party of King Charles; it is now, I believe, considered equally grotesque, on moral grounds, to be of the party of the Puritans; and to most persons to-day the religious views of both parties may seem equally remote. Nevertheless, the passions are unquenched, and if we are not very wide awake their smoke will obscure the glass through which we examine Milton's poetry. Something has been done, certainly, to persuade us that Milton was never really of any party, but disagreed with everyone. Mr. Wilson Knight, in *Chariot of Wrath*, has argued that Milton was more a monarchist than a republican, and not in any modern sense a 'democrat,' and Professor Saurat has produced evidence to show that Milton's theology was highly eccentric, and as scandalous to Protestants as to Catholics—that he was, in fact, a sort of Christadelphian, and perhaps not a very orthodox Christadelphian at that; while on the other hand Mr. C. S. Lewis has opposed Professor Saurat by skilfully arguing that Milton, at least in *Paradise Lost*, can be acquitted of heresy even from a point of view so orthodox as that of Mr. Lewis himself. On these questions I hold no opinion: it is probably beneficial to question the assumption that Milton was a sound Free Churchman and member of the Liberal Party; but I think that we still have to be on guard against an unconscious partisanship if we aim to attend to the poetry for the poetry's sake.

So much for our prejudices. I come next to the positive objection to Milton which has been raised in our own time, that is to say, the charge that he is an unwholesome influence. And from this I shall proceed to the permanent strictures of reproof [to employ a phrase of Johnson's] and, finally, to the grounds on which I consider him a great poet and one whom poets to-day might study with profit.

For a statement of the *generalized* belief in the unwholesomeness of Milton's influence I turn to Mr. Middleton Murry's critique of Milton in his Heaven and Earth—a book which contains chapters of profound insight, interrupted by passages which seem to me intemperate. Mr. Murry approaches Milton after his long and patient study of Keats; and it is through the eyes of Keats that he sees Milton.

'Keats [*Mr. Murry writes*] as a poetic artist, second to none since Shakespeare, and Blake, as a prophet of spiritual values unique in our history, both passed substantially the same judgement on Milton: "Life to him would be death to me." And whatever may be our verdict on the development of English poetry, since Milton, we must admit the justice of Keats's opinion that Milton's magnificence led nowhere. "English must be kept up," said Keats. To be influenced beyond a certain point by Milton's art, be felt, dammed the creative flow of the English genius in and through itself. In saying this, I think, Keats voiced the very inmost of the English genius. To pass under the spell of Milton is to be condemned to imitate him. It is quite different with Shakespeare. Shakespeare baffles and liberates; Milton is perspicuous and constricts.'

This is a very confident affirmation, and I criticize it with some diffidence because I cannot pretend to have devoted as much study to Keats, or to have as intimate an understanding of his difficulties, as Mr. Murry. But Mr. Murry seems to me here to be trying to transform the predicament of a particular poet with a particular aim at a particular moment in time into a censure of timeless validity. He appears to assert that the liberative function of Shakespeare and the constrictive menace of Milton are permanent characteristics of these two poets. 'To be influenced beyond a certain point' by any one master is bad for any poet; and it does not matter whether that influence is Milton's or another's; and as we cannot anticipate where that point will come, we might be better advised to call it an uncertain point. If it is not good to remain under the spell of Milton, is it good to remain under the spell of Shakespeare? It depends partly upon what *genre* of poetry you are trying to develop. Keats wanted to write an epic, and he found, as might be expected, that the time had not arrived at which another English epic, comparable in grandeur to *Paradise Lost*, could be written. He also tried his hand at writing plays: and one might argue that *King Stephen* was more blighted by Shakespeare than *Hyperion* by Milton. Certainly, *Hyperion* remains a magnificent fragment which one re-reads; and *King Stephen* is a play which we may have read once, but to which we never return for enjoyment, Milton made a great epic impossible for succeeding generations; Shakespeare made a great poetic drama impossible; such a situation is inevitable, and it persists until the language has so altered that there is no danger, because no possibility, of imitation. Anyone who tries to write poetic drama, even to-day, should know that half of his energy must be exhausted in the effort to escape from the constricting toils of Shakespeare: the moment his attention is relaxed, or his mind fatigued, he will lapse into bad Shakespearian verse. For a long time after an epic poet like Milton, or a dramatic poet like Shakespeare, nothing can be done. Yet the effort must be repeatedly made; for we can never know in advance when the moment is approaching at which a new epic, or a new drama, will be possible; and when the moment does draw near it may be that the genius of an individual poet will perform the last mutation of idiom and versification which will bring that new poetry into being.

I have referred to Mr. Murry's view of the bad influence of Milton as generalized, because it is implicitly the whole personality of Milton that is in question: not specifically his beliefs, or his language or versification, but the beliefs as realized in that particular personality, and his poetry as the expression of it. By the *particular* view of Milton's influence as bad, I mean that view which attends to the language, the syntax, the versification, the imagery. I do not suggest that there is here a complete difference of subject matter: it is the difference of approach, the difference of the focus of interest, between the philosophical critic and the literary critic. An incapacity for the abstruse, and an interest in poetry which is primarily a technical interest, dispose my mind towards the more limited and perhaps more superficial task. Let us proceed to look at Milton's influence from this point of view, that of the writer of poetry in our own time.

The reproach against Milton, that his technical influence has been bad, appears to have been made by no one more positively than by myself. I find myself saying, as recently as 1936, that this charge against Milton 'appears a good deal more serious if we affirm that Milton's poetry could *only* be an influence for the worse, upon any poet whatever. It is more serious, also, if we affirm that Milton's bad influence may be traced much farther than the eighteenth century, and much farther than upon bad poets: if we say that it was an influence against which we still have to struggle'

In writing these sentences I failed to draw a threefold distinction, which now seems to me of some importance. There are three separate assertions implied. The first is, that an influence has been bad in the past: this is to assert that good poets, in the eighteenth or nineteenth century, would have written better if they had not submitted themselves to the influence of Milton. The second assertion is, that the contemporary situation is such that Milton is a master whom we should avoid. The third is, that the influence of Milton, or of any particular poet, can be *always* bad, and that we can predict that wherever it is found at any time in the future, however remote, it will be a bad influence. Now, the first and third of these assertions I am no longer prepared to make, because, detached from the second, they do not appear to me to have any meaning.

For the first, when we consider one great poet of the past, and one or more other poets, upon whom we say he has exerted a bad influence, we must admit that the responsibility, if there be any, is rather with the poets who were influenced than with the poet whose work exerted the influence. We can, of course, show that certain tricks or mannerisms which the imitators display are due to conscious or unconscious imitation and emulation, but that is a reproach against their injudicious choice of a model and not against their model itself. And we can never prove that any particular poet would have written better poetry if he had escaped that influence. Even if we assert, what can only be a matter of faith, that Keats would have written a very great epic poem if Milton had not preceded him, is it sensible to pine for an unwritten masterpiece, in exchange for one which we possess and acknowledge? And as for the remote future, what can we affirm about the poetry that will be written then, except that we should probably be unable to understand or to enjoy it, and that therefore we can hold no opinion as to what 'good' and 'bad' influences will mean in that future? The only relation in which the question of influence, good and bad, is significant, is the relation to the immediate future. With that question I shall engage at the end. I wish first to mention another reproach against Milton, that represented by the phrase 'dissociation of sensibility'.

I remarked many years ago, in an essay on Dryden, that:

'In the seventeenth century a dissociation of sensibility set in, from which we have never recovered; and this dissociation, as is natural, was due to the influence of the two most powerful poets of the century, Milton and Dryden.'

The longer passage from which this sentence is taken is quoted by Dr. Tillyard in his *Milton*. Dr. Tillyard makes the following comment:

'Speaking only of what in this passage concerns Milton, I would say that there is here a mixture of truth and falsehood. Some sort of dissociation of sensibility in Milton, not necessarily undesirable, has to be admitted; but that he was responsible for any such dissociation in others [at least till this general dissociation had inevitably set in] is untrue.'

I believe that the general affirmation represented by the phrase 'dissociation of sensibility' [one of the two or three phrases of my coinage—like 'objective correlative'—which have had a success in the world astonishing to their author] retains some validity; but I now incline to agree with Dr. Tillyard that to lay the burden on the shoulders of Milton and Dryden was a mistake. If such a dissociation did take place, I suspect that the causes are too complex and too profound to justify our accounting for the change in terms of literary criticism. All we can say is that something like this did happen; that it had something to do with the Civil War; that it would even be unwise to say it was caused by the Civil War, but that it is a consequence of the same causes which brought about the Civil War; that we must seek the causes in Europe, not in England alone; and for what these causes were, we may dig—and dig until we get to a depth at which words and concepts fail us.

Before proceeding to take up the case against Milton, as it stood for poets twenty-five years ago—the second, and only significant meaning of 'bad influence'—I think it would be best to consider what permanent strictures of reproof may be drawn: those censures which, when we make them, we must assume to be made by enduring laws of taste. The essence of the permanent censure of Milton is, I believe, to be found in Johnson's essay. This is not the place in which to examine certain particular and erroneous judgments of Johnson; to explain his condemnation of *Comus* and *Samson* as the application of dramatic canons which to us seem inapplicable; or to condone his dismissal of the versification of *Lycidas* by the specialization, rather than the absence, of his sense of rhythm. Johnson's most important censure of Milton is contained in three paragraphs, which I must ask leave to quote in full.

'Throughout all his greater works [*says Johnson*] there prevails an uniform peculiarity of *diction*, a mode and cast of expression which bears little resemblance to that of any former writer; and which is so far removed from common use, that an unlearned reader, when he first opens the book, finds himself surprised by a new language.

'This novelty has been, by those who can find nothing wrong with Milton, imputed to his laborious endeavours after words suited to the grandeur of his ideas. *Our language*, says Addison, *sunk under him*. But the truth is, that both in prose and in verse, he had formed his style by a perverse and pedantic principle. He was desirous to use English words with a foreign idiom. This in all his prose is discovered and condemned; for there judgment operates freely, neither softened by the beauty, nor awed by the dignity of his thoughts; but such is the power of his poetry, that his call is obeyed without resistance, the reader feels himself in captivity to a higher and nobler mind, and criticism sinks in admiration.

'Milton's style was not modified by his subject; what is shown with greater extent in *Paradise Lost* may be found in *Comus*. One source of his peculiarity was his familiarity with the Tuscan poets; the disposition of his words is, I think, frequently Italian; perhaps sometimes combined with other tongues. Of him at last, may be said what Jonson said of Spenser, that he *wrote no language*, but has formed what Butler called a *Babylonish dialect*, in itself harsh and barbarous, but made by exalted genius and extensive learning the vehicle of so much instruction and so much pleasure, that, like other lovers, we find grace in its deformity.'

This criticism seems to me substantially true: indeed, unless we accept it, I do not think we are in the way to appreciate the peculiar greatness of Milton. His style is not a *classic* style, in that it is not the elevation of a *common* style, by the final touch of genius, to greatness. It is, from the foundation, and in every particular, a personal style, not based upon common speech, or common prose, or direct communication of meaning. Of some great poetry one has difficulty in pronouncing just what it is, what infinitesimal touch, that has made all the difference from a plain statement which anyone could make; the slight transformation which, while it leaves a plain statement a plain statement, has always the maximal, never the minimal, alteration of ordinary language. Every distortion of construction, the foreign idiom, the use of a word in a foreign way or with the meaning of the foreign word from which it is derived rather than the accepted meaning in English, every idiosyncrasy is a particular act of violence which Milton has been the first to commit. There is no cliché, no poetic diction in the derogatory sense, but a perpetual sequence of original acts of lawlessness. Of all modern writers of verse, the nearest analogy seems to me to be Mallarmé, a much smaller poet, though still a great one. The personalities, the poetic theories of the two men could not have been more different; but in respect of the violence which they could do to language, and justify, there is a remote similarity. Milton's poetry is poetry as the farthest possible remove from prose; his prose seems to me too near to half-formed poetry to be a good prose.

To say that the work of a poet is at the farthest possible remove from prose would once have struck me as condemnatory: it now seems to me simply, when we have to do with a Milton, the precision of its peculiar greatness. As a poet, Milton seems to me probably the greatest of all eccentrics. His work illustrates no general principles of good writing; the only principles of writing that it illustrates are such as are valid only for Milton himself to observe. There are two kinds of poet who can ordinarily be of use to other poets. There are those who suggest, to one or another of their successors, something which they have not done themselves, or who provoke a different way of doing the same thing: these are likely to be not the greatest, but smaller, imperfect poets with whom later poets discover an affinity. And there are the great poets from whom we can learn negative rules: no poet can teach another to write well, but some great poets can teach others some of the things to avoid. They teach us what to avoid, by showing us what great poetry can do without—how *bare* it can be. Of these are Dante and Racine. But if we are ever to make use of Milton we must do so in quite a different way. Even a small poet can learn something from the study of Dante, or from the study of Chaucer: we must perhaps wait for a great poet before we find one who can profit from the study of Milton.

I repeat that the remoteness of Milton's verse from ordinary speech, his invention of his own poetic language, seems to me one of the marks of his greatness. Other marks are his sense of structure, both in the general design of *Paradise Lost* and *Samson*, and in his syntax; and finally, and not least, his inerrancy, conscious or unconscious, in writing so as to make the best display of his talents, and the best concealment of his weaknesses.

The appropriateness of the subject of *Samson* is too obvious to expatiate upon: it was probably the one dramatic story out of which Milton could have made a masterpiece. But the complete suitability of *Paradise Lost* has not, I think, been so often remarked. It was surely an intuitive perception of what he could not do, that arrested Milton's project of an epic on King Arthur. For one thing, he had little interest in, or understanding of, individual human beings. In *Paradise Lost* he was not called upon for any of that understanding which comes from an affectionate observation of men and women. But such an interest in human beings was not required—indeed its *absence* was a necessary condition—for the creation of his figures of Adam and Eve. These are not a man and woman such as any we know: if they were, they would not be Adam and Eve. They are the original *Man* and *Woman*, not types, but prototypes. They have the general characteristics of men and women, such that we can recognize, in the temptation and the fall, the first motions of the faults and virtues, the abjection and the nobility, of all their descendants. They have ordinary humanity to the right degree, and yet are not, and should not be, ordinary mortals. Were they more particularized they would be false, and if Milton had been more interested in humanity, he could not have created them. Other critics have remarked upon the exactness, without defect or exaggeration, with which Moloch, Belial, and Mammon, in the second book, speak according to the particular sin which each represents. It would not be suitable that the infernal powers should have, in the human sense, characters, for a character is always mixed; but in the hands of an inferior manipulator, they might easily have been reduced to *humours*.

The appropriateness of the material of *Paradise Lost* to the genius and the limitations of Milton is still more evident when we consider the visual imagery. I have already remarked, in a paper written some years ago, on Milton's weakness of visual observation, a weakness which I think was always present—the effect of his blindness may have been rather to strengthen the compensatory qualities than to increase a fault which was already present. Mr. Wilson Knight, who has devoted close study to recurrent imagery in poetry, has called attention to Milton's propensity towards images of engineering and mechanics; to me it seems that Milton is at his best in imagery suggestive of vast size, limitless space, abysmal depth, and light and darkness. No theme and no setting, other than that which he chose in *Paradise Lost*, could have given him such scope for the kind of imagery in which he excelled, or made less demand upon those powers of visual imagination which were in him defective.

Most of the absurdities and inconsistencies to which Johnson calls attention, and which, so far as they can justly be isolated in this way, he properly condemns, will I think appear in a more correct proportion if we consider them in relation to this general judgment. I do not think that we should attempt to *see* very clearly any scene that Milton depicts: it should be accepted as a shifting phantasmagory. To complain, because we first find the arch-fiend 'chain'd on the burning lake', and in a minute or two see him making his way to the shore, is to expect a kind of consistency which the world to which Milton has introduced us does not require.

This limitation of visual power, like Milton's limited interest in human beings, turns out to be not merely a negligible defect, but a positive virtue, when we visit Adam and Eve in Eden. Just as a higher degree of characterization of Adam and Eve would have been unsuitable, so a more vivid picture of the earthly Paradise would have been less paradisiacal. For a greater definiteness, a more detailed account of flora and fauna, could only have assimilated Eden to the landscapes of earth with which we are familiar. As it is, the impression of Eden which we retain, is the most suitable, and is that which Milton was most qualified to give: the impression of *light*—a daylight and a starlight, a light of dawn and of dusk, the light which, remembered by a man in his blindness, has a supernatural glory unexperienced by men of normal vision.

We must, then, in reading *Paradise Lost*, not expect to see clearly; our sense of sight must be blurred, so that our *hearing* may become more acute. *Paradise Lost*, like *Finnegans Wake* [for I can think of no work which provides a more interesting parallel: two books by great blind musicians, each writing a language of his own based upon English] makes this peculiar demand for a readjustment of the reader's mode of apprehension. The emphasis is on the sound, not the vision, upon the word, not the idea; and in the end it is the unique versification that is the most certain sign of Milton's intellectual mastership.

On the subject of Milton's versification, so far as I am aware, little enough has been written. We have Johnson's essay in the *Rambler*, which deserves more study than it has received, and we have a short treatise by Robert Bridges on *Milton's Prosody*. I speak of Bridges with respect, for no poet of our time has given such close attention to prosody as he. Bridges catalogues the systematic irregularities which give perpetual variety to Milton's verse, and I can find no fault with his analysis. But however interesting these analyses are, I do not think that it is by such means that we gain an appreciation of the peculiar rhythm of a poet. It seems to me also that Milton's verse is especially refractory to yielding up its secrets to examination of the single line. For his verse is not formed in this way. It is the period, the sentence and still more the paragraph, that is the unit of Milton's verse; and emphasis on the line structure is the minimum necessary to provide a counter-pattern to the period structure. It is only in the period that the wavelength of Milton's verse is to be found: it is his ability to give a perfect and unique pattern to every paragraph, such that the full beauty of the line is found in its context, and his ability to work in larger musical units than any other poet—that is to me the most conclusive evidence of Milton's supreme mastery. The peculiar feeling, almost a physical sensation of a breathless leap, communicated by Milton's long periods, and by his alone, is impossible to procure from rhymed verse. Indeed, this mastery is more conclusive evidence of his intellectual power, than is his grasp of any *ideas* that he borrowed or invented. To be able to control so many words at once is the token of a mind of most exceptional energy.

It is interesting at this point to recall the general observations upon blank verse, which a consideration of *Paradise Lost* prompted Johnson to make towards the end of his essay.

'The music of the English heroic lines strikes the ear so faintly, that it is easily lost, unless all the syllables of every line co-operate together; this co-operation can only be obtained by the preservation of every verse unmingled with another as a distinct system of sounds; and this distinctness is obtained and preserved by the artifice of rhyme. The variety of pauses, so much boasted by the lovers of blank verse, changes the measures of an English poet to the periods of a declaimer; and there are only a few skilful and happy readers of Milton, who enable their audience to perceive where the lines end or begin. *Blank verse*, said an ingenious critic, *seems to be verse only to the eye.*'

Some of my audience may recall that this last remark, in almost the same words, was often made, a literary generation ago, about the 'free verse' of the period: and even without this encouragement from Johnson it would have occurred to my mind to declare Milton to be the greatest master of free verse in our language. What is interesting about Johnson's paragraph, however, is that it represents the judgment of a man who had by no means a deaf ear, but simply a *specialized* ear, for verbal music. Within the limits of the poetry of his own period, Johnson is a very good judge of the relative merits of several poets as writers of blank verse. But on the whole, the blank verse of his age might more properly be called unrhymed verse; and nowhere is this difference more evident than in the verse of his own tragedy *Irene*: the phrasing is admirable, the style elevated and correct, but each line cries out for a companion to rhyme with it. Indeed, it is only with labour, or by occasional inspiration, or by submission to the influence of the older dramatists, that the blank verse of the nineteenth century succeeds in making the absence of rhyme inevitable and right, with the rightness of Milton. Even Johnson admitted that he could not wish that Milton had been a rhymer. Nor did the nineteenth century succeed in giving to blank verse the flexibility which it needs if the tone of common speech, talking of the topics of common intercourse, is to be employed; so that when our more modern practitioners of blank verse do not touch the sublime, they frequently sink to the ridiculous. Milton perfected non-dramatic blank verse and at the same time imposed limitations, very hard to break, upon the use to which it may be put if its greatest musical possibilities are to be exploited.

I come at last to compare my own attitude, as that of a poetical practitioner perhaps typical of a generation twenty-five years ago, with my attitude to-day. I have thought it well to take matters in the order in which I have taken them to discuss first the censures and detractions which I believe to have permanent validity, and which were best made by Johnson, in order to make clearer the causes, and the justification, for hostility to Milton on the part of poets at a particular juncture. And I wished to make clear those excellences of Milton which particularly impress me, before explaining why I think that the study of his verse might at last be of benefit to poets.

I have on several occasions suggested, that the important changes in the idiom of English verse which are represented by the names of Dryden and Wordsworth, may be characterized as successful attempts to escape from a poetic idiom which had ceased to have a relation to contemporary speech. This is the sense of Wordsworth's Prefaces. By the beginning of the present century another revolution in idiom—and such revolutions bring with them an alteration of metric, a new appeal to the ear—was due. It inevitably happens that the young poets engaged in such a revolution will exalt the merits of those poets of the past who offer them example and stimulation, and cry down the merits of poets who do not stand for the qualities which they are zealous to realize. This is not only inevitable, it is right. It is even right, and certainly inevitable, that their practice, still more influential than their critical pronouncements, should attract their own readers to the poets by whose work they have been influenced. Such influence has certainly contributed to the taste [if we can distinguish the *taste* from the *fashion*] for Donne. I do not think that any modern poet, unless in a fit of irresponsible peevishness, has ever denied Milton's consummate powers. And it must be said that Milton's diction is not a poetic diction in the sense of being a debased currency: when he violates the English language he is imitating nobody, and he is inimitable. But Milton does, as I have said, represent poetry at the extreme limit from prose; and it was one of our tenets that verse should have the virtues of prose, that diction should become assimilated to cultivated contemporary speech, before aspiring to the elevation of poetry. Another tenet was that the subject-matter and the imagery of poetry should be extended to topics and objects related to the life of a modern man or woman; that we were to seek the non-poetic, to seek even material refractory to transmutation into poetry, and words and phrases which had not been used in poetry before. And the study of Milton could be of no help here: it was only a hindrance.

We cannot, in literature, any more than in the rest of life, live in a perpetual state of revolution. If every generation of poets made it their task to bring poetic diction up to date with the spoken language, poetry would fail in one of its most important obligations. For poetry should help, not only to refine the language of the time, but to prevent it from changing too rapidly: a development of language at too great a speed would be a development in the sense of a progressive deterioration, and that is our danger to-day. If the poetry of the rest of this century takes the line of development which seems to me, reviewing the progress of poetry through the last three centuries, the right course, it will discover new and more elaborate patterns of a diction now established. In this search it might have much to learn from Milton's extended verse structure; it might also avoid the danger of a servitude to colloquial speech and to current jargon. It might also learn that the music of verse is strongest in poetry which has a definite meaning expressed in the properest words. Poets might be led to admit that a knowledge of the literature of their own language, with a knowledge of the literature and the grammatical construction of other languages, is a very valuable part of the poet's equipment. And they might, as I have already hinted, devote some study to Milton as, outside the theatre, the greatest master in our language of freedom within form. A study of *Samson* should sharpen anyone's appreciation of the justified irregularity, and put him on guard against the pointless irregularity. In studying *Paradise Lost* we come to perceive that the verse is continuously animated by the departure from, and return to, the regular measure; and that, in comparison with Milton, hardly any subsequent writer of blank verse appears to exercise any freedom at all. We can also be led to the reflection that a monotony of unscannable verse fatigues the attention even more quickly than a monotony of exact feet. In short, it now seems to me that Poets are sufficiently liberated from Milton's reputation, to approach the study of his work without danger, and with profit to their poetry and to the English language.

STANLEY EUGENE FISH

The Interpretative Choice

I. VAIN SPECULATIONS

Wondering at the 'blind alleys' readers of *Paradise Lost* have been led into, C. S. Lewis moves to 'dismiss that question which has so much agitated some great critics, "What is the Fall?"' by answering, 'The Fall is simply and solely Disobedience—doing what you have been told not to do.' Aligning himself with Addison, for whom 'the great moral which reigns in Milton is ... Obedience to the will of God makes men happy', Lewis poses a question of his own: 'How are we to account for the fact that great modern scholars have missed what is so dazzlingly simple?'[1] This could be profitably rephrased to read, 'How are we to account for the fact that Adam and Eve, when the time comes, miss what is so dazzlingly simple?' For the reader, the poem is a 'life situation', analogous to the situation of the happy couple in Paradise. The 'dazzling simplicity' of the poem's great moral is the counterpart of the dazzlingly simple prohibition, and the obligation of the parties in the two situations is to defend the starkness of the moral choice against sophistications which seem to make disobedience attractive ('Here grows the Cure of all, this Fruit Divine') or necessary ('what seem'd remediless'). The opportunities to yield to such sophistications are provided by God and Milton, respectively, who wish to try the faith and integrity of their

---

From *Surprised by Sin: the Reader in Paradise Lost* by Stanley Fish: pp. 208-240. Published by the University of California Press. © 1967 by Stanley Fish. Reprinted by permission.

charges. Lewis hopes to 'prevent the reader from ever raising certain questions', but Milton insists that the reader raise them, and then that he answer them, either by recalling the simplicity of the revealed word or by turning inward where there are waiting a ready supply of self-serving rationalizations. These rationalizations become screens behind which the reader may hide from himself facts he finds unpleasant, notably the fact of man's culpability for what happened in Paradise and since. But he is free, on the other hand, to decline the gambit and accept instead the 'desolating clarity' of 'For still they knew, and ought to have still remember'd / The high Injunction not to taste that Fruit' (x. 12–13). Whatever he decides, it is his responsibility, as it was theirs.

Mrs. MacCaffrey observes that in describing the intellectual vanity of the fallen angels, 'Milton is describing *human* preoccupations.' Philosophy may be false, 'but humanity will go on philosophizing'.[2] Certainly the reader will go on philosophizing, and his *concerns*, as the critical history of the poem proves, are the same as the devils'

> Of Providence, Foreknowledge, Will, and Fate,
> Fixt Fate, Free will, Foreknowledge absolute,
> And found no end, in wand'ring mazes lost,
> Of good and evil much they argu'd then,
> Of happiness and final misery,
> Passion and Apathy, and glory and shame,
> Vain wisdom all, and false Philosophy:
> Yet with a pleasing sorcery could charm
> Pain for a while.
> (ll. 559-67)

How does one reconcile freedom of will with the absolute foreknowledge of the Creator? How can actions which have been foreseen be free? How can evil proceed from a perfectly good being? The declarative forms of these questions are the staples of anti-Milton criticism:

(1) *Adam and Eve were fated to fall*. 'I do not see what the incident can mean except that God was determined to make man fall.' (Empson, *Milton's God*, p. 112.)

(2) *Their disobedience, as we see it, is determined, partly by circumstances, partly by their own natures*. 'Man yields to temptation when he is caught in an archetypal net of circumstance and mixed motivation, from which,

being what he is, no amount of faith or foreknowledge can extricate him.... The enmeshing of the victims is so beautifully contrived ... human nature as much as Satan undoes Adam and Eve.' (Watkins, *An Anatomy of Milton's Verse*, p. 141.)

(3) *They were created with a propensity to fall.* 'If they could fall, were they not already in some sense fallen?' (Ricks, *Milton's Grand Style*, p. 99.)³ Obviously these arguments represent slightly different paths to the same conclusion: God, not Adam and Eve, is guilty of the Fall, and curiously enough, it is God himself who raises them by gratuitously refuting them:

> nor can justly accuse
> Thir maker, or thir making, or thir Fate;
> As if Predestination over-rul'd
> Thir will, dispos'd by absolute Decree
> Or high foreknowledge; they themselves decreed
> Thir own revolt, not I: if I foreknew,
> Foreknowledge had no influence on their fault,
> Which had no less provd certain unforeknown.
> So without least impulse or shadow of Fate,
> Or aught by me immutably foreseen,
> They trespass, Authors to themselves in all
> Both what they judge and what they choose; for so
> I form'd them free, and free they must remain,
> Till they enthrall themselves—I else must change
> Thir nature, and revoke the high Decree
> Unchangeable, Eternal, which ordain'd
> Thir freedom: they themselves ordain'd thir *fall*.
> (III. 112–28)

These assertions are made in the course of a methodical exposition to which the speaker expects no response; but the effect on his audience of eavesdroppers is to suggest 'inventions' by means of which the Fall can be circumvented. As David Daiches points out (not in praise, however), 'the reader, however much he wishes to read *Paradise Lost* "as a poem," is forced to read it at this point as logical argument, and to answer back as he reads.'⁴ Whether or not he 'answers back', in the sense of disagreeing, the reader will be unable to ignore the difficulties involved in the logic of foreknowledge and freedom. These difficulties are acknowledged (not personally, but as part of a logical proof) by God, and resolved; but the reader will have been exposed to the attractiveness of the evasions God disallows—I ordained their Fall, the shadow of Fate hangs over them, they were not 'sufficient to have stood'—and thereafter, whenever an innocent detail is capable of being twisted so that it seems to forebode the Fall, whenever an isolated incident can be (illegitimately) structured into a 'net of circumstance', whenever Adam and Eve evidence their ability to fall (the necessary complement of their ability not to fall), these evasions, in all their seductiveness, are recalled, and, if we allow them, they undermine our understanding of the situation as God and Milton have instituted it.

Undoubtedly, by eliminating some passages and altering the emphasis of others, Milton could have neutralized the 'pleasing sorcery' of these speculations. That he did not choose to do so is less an indication of a deficiency in tact than of a willingness to risk all in order to bring the reader to self-awareness. One may be proof against the obvious temptations of the world, the flesh and the devil, but fall to the promptings of the enemy within, to 'the secret deceit which we perceive not' but which is working all the while in the 'many blinde corners, the ... turnings and windings, the perplexe labrynths'[5] of the human heart. 'In clearing ourselves when guilty', warns Dyke, 'the heart of man is so subtle that if it can finde out any other thing or person, that in the least sort may seem to be but the least peece of an occasion, that shall be sufficient to free itselfe of all manner of blame.'[6] (Significantly, one 'tricke' discussed by Dyke is the imputing of sin to God.[7]) Milton forces to the surface the deceitful and self-serving thoughts ('the wily suttleties and refluxes ... from within')[8] employed by the subconscious to avoid uncomfortable truths, and insists that they be submitted to the correction and judgment of the revealed word. Of course, since these thoughts are manifestations of a desire to escape judgment ('Self-love makes one rather excuse what is amiss, than examine it'),[9] the reader may persist in them, even when their subversiveness has been made apparent; but he will at least be conscious of his temerity in affirming against the authority of the poet and scripture.[10]

The result is a reading experience which has been described, disapprovingly, by Waldock: 'our reception of a given passage can be, and often is, a blend of two things: what we have really read in the passage, and what we know Milton is wishing us to read into it' (op. cit., p. 26). I would say instead that our reception is a blend of what, for various reasons, we would like to read into the passage, and what we know, from unimpeachable sources, is really there. So that in any one scene, including the crucial scenes of Book IX, there are available two interpretations; one, urged on us by the epic voice or by our own awareness of the possibilities and their implications, supports and gives body to the picture of Edenic reality outlined by God in Book III, while the other points, however indirectly, to his villainy and our parents' (technical) innocence.

As before, the subversive response (interpretation) is first encouraged and then discredited, leaving the reader to come to terms with the appeal it has for him. At III. 127, when God declares his unwillingness to 'revoke the high Decree / ... which ordain'd / Thir freedom', the reader is likely to extend the influence of the decree to the Fall which is also assumed to be ordained; but immediately, as if he were anticipating in advance the 'wily suttleties' of the fallen mind, God insists, 'they themselves ordain'd thir Fall'.[11] The possibility of disbelieving him still exists, but disbelief can be maintained only in the face of God's faultless logic which can be understood if the reader is willing to make the effort. There are then two choices before the reader (1) whether or not to work through the apparent contradiction between foreknowledge and freedom to an understanding of the distinction between what will happen and what must happen (2) whether or not to reject completely the alternative reading which has the advantage (from a 'selfish' point of view) of excusing the frailty of his first parents,[12] and, by extension, his own frailties. In the middle books (IV–IX) these same choices are structured into a series of scenes which provide a continuing test of the reader's steadfastness and honesty. The technique is again the technique of the 'good temptation' whereby the reader is left to choose, in a controlled situation, which of two roads he will take. That is to say, the interpretative choice—which is to be distinguished from the 'responsive choice' in that it requires a decision concerning the meaning of an action or a scene, and so affects the reader's understanding of the poem itself—is always made consciously and wilfully, and is ultimately a choice between the word of God and the structures reared (self-defensively) by the reader's reason.

II. THE CHOICES

In Book IV, when Eve recalls her early life without Adam, the choice is between two readings of the allusion to Narcissus:

> Not distant far from thence a murmuring sound
> Of waters issu'd from a Cave and spread
> Into a liquid Plain, then stood unmov'd
> Pure as th' expanse of Heav'n; I thither went
> With unexperienc't thought, and laid me down
> On the green bank, to look into the clear
> Smooth Lake, that to me seem'd another Sky.
> As I bent down to look, just opposite,
> A Shape within the wat'ry gleam appear'd
> Bending to look on me, I started back,
> It started back, but pleas'd I soon return'd,
> Pleas'd it returned as soon with answering looks
> Of sympathy and love; there I had fixt
> Mine eyes till now, and pin'd with vain desire
> Had not a voice thus warn'd me.
> (4.53–67)

One can either conclude with Mrs. Bell that 'we have glimpsed a dainty vanity in "our general mother" which the serpent will put to use', or contrive, with Peter and Harding, to disengage her from the pejorative connotations of the myth:

> The incident is actually one of the most engaging glimpses we have of Eve's artless [innocent] simplicity ... and the childlike honesty with which she compares the physical appearances of Adam and herself is wholly disarming.
>
> Eve is saved, as Narcissus is not, by a warning voice, and it would be a captious reader indeed who ... would be inclined to read too much into this.[13]

There is much in the text itself to support Peter and Harding. 'Childlike' (or, better still, infantlike) seems perfectly true to the reaction Eve displays to her newly discovered image: the curiosity—'I thither went / With unexperienc't thought'—the movement back and forth—'I started back, / It started back, but pleas'd I soon return'd' (the patterned repetitions lead the reader to imitate the motion)—and the (innocent) fascination—'there I had fixt / Mine eyes'. And Eve's yielding to Adam would seem to indicate, as Harding implies and Summers insists, that 'the point ... is the contrast rather than the comparison with ... Narcissus':

> Narcissus had no 'perfect' partner, no 'other self', and he had no divine guide...she *has* found fulfillment,...she had not 'pin'd with vain desire'.[14]

In addition, one should note that, in telling her story, Eve, far from 'unexperienc't', is mature in wisdom; she is now aware, as she may not have been before, of the true significance of her yielding:

> I yielded, and from that time see
> How beauty is excell'd by manly grace
> And wisdom, which alone is truly fair.
> (489–91)

This is obviously 'the professed moral of the episode'.[15]

The possibility, however, of *not* reaching for the contrast (an effort is required) and *not* crediting her maturity still remains. Ignoring the evidence to the contrary, evidence Milton is always careful to provide, the reader, whose will is also free, may decide to disbelieve Eve, looking no further than the surface parallel, and thus begin to ease, conscious at some level of the error, into the opinion 'that Adam and Eve must have already contracted ... weaknesses before they can start on the course of conduct that leads to their fall.[16] (Of course, if the will is free, *no* course of conduct can *lead* to the Fall which is a spontaneous, i.e. free, action.) What the reader cannot possibly do is ignore the problem (the eighteenth-century commentators were already debating it)[17] once the Ovidian allusion is recognized. The presence of Narcissus, even at a remove, is a puzzle, which, like the literal incongruity of some parts of scripture and the appearance during the creation scene of the phrase 'With Serpent error wand'ring', is designed to exercise the reader's mind and to present him with a choice he cannot avoid.

The same pattern is repeated on a larger scale in the episode of Eve's dream, where the suggestion of a tainted consciousness is at odds with the moral drawn by Adam. The suggestion is conveyed to the reader in Book IV, when Satan is seen 'Assaying ... / ... if inspiring venom, he might taint / Th' animal spirits that from pure blood arise / ... thence raise / At least distemper'd, discontented thoughts, / Vain hopes, vain aims, inordinate desires / Blown up with high conceits ingend'ring pride' (IV. 801, 804–9). Presumably, this is the basis of a reading like Northrop Frye's:

> The occasion of her dream was Satan whispering in her ear; but the dream itself, in its manifest content, was a Freudian wish-fulfilment dream.[18]

Notice that Frye assumes Satan's success, while the verse itself leaves the matter in doubt. Satan is *assaying* to reach her Fancy, in the hope that he could then 'forge / Illusions as he list;' or, barring that, he will see *if* he can infuse venom into her *which* might then taint her animal spirits. There is more than a hint that his calculations may prove incorrect. Of course, a careless reader, or one who is eager to find trouble in Paradise, can easily detach 'Blown up with high conceits ingend'ring pride' from the syntax of the paragraph (Milton allows him that latitude) and accept the line as a statement of fact, applicable to Eve as she sleeps. He would, however, be guilty of a (wilful) distortion.

A more reliable insight into Eve's state of mind is provided, somewhat indirectly I admit, in the word 'startl'd':

'Such whispering wak'd her, but with startl'd eye.' (V. 26) In *Comus*, the Lady, oppressed by 'A thousand fantasies / ... Of calling shapes and beck'ning shadows dire', waking fancies not unlike Eve's, declares forthrightly: 'These thoughts may startle well, but not astound / The virtuous mind' (210–11). The virtuous mind may be surprised (startled) by an untoward suggestion without surrendering to it. And even if the body is under evil's spell, as Eve's is here and will be again when she follows the serpent to the tree, the virtuous mind is still able to assert itself:

> Thou canst not touch the freedom of my mind
> ... although this corporal rind
> Thou hast immanacl'd.
>   (*Comus*, 663–5)

This is the point Adam will make when he explains to Eve the significance of her dream, and it is one we should be prepared to understand.[19]

The dream is a carefully woven web of echoing and anticipatory detail. Satan's opening 'Why sleep'st thou Eve' is a slightly altered version of his 'earlier' address to Beelzebub, 'Sleep'st thou companion dear?' (673). (The relationship between the two temptations is confused for us since we have not yet been told of the revolt which has already occurred when Satan squats at the ear of Eve.) His first appeal is a parody of Adam's parody of *The Song of Songs*, with a significant difference: Adam invites Eve to enjoy the wonders of God's nature, 'Awake, the morning shines and the fresh field / Calls us' (20–21); Satan invites her to be worshipped, 'Heaven wakes with all his eyes, / Whom to behold but thee?' (44–45). Is this merely another instance, we ask, of the fiend's inability to imagine motives not rooted in self-love, or is it that he knows Eve better than Adam does and can fashion an argument which will sway her? The answer any reader gives will depend to some extent on the meaning he has assigned to the incident at the pool. The angel whose dewy locks distil ambrosia is of course Satan as he was in the meeting with Uriel. Does one deception have any bearing on the probable success of the other? The question will certainly raise itself, and again, the answer will depend on the care the reader is willing to exercise in the drawing of conclusions.

Satan's approach is leisurely, as it will be in Book IX. Flattery ('fair Angelic *Eve*') and Godhead ('be henceforth among the Gods') are the twin prongs of his strategy, merging in a final appeal, 'Ascend to Heav'n, by merit thine' (80). The logic is familiar, as it has been rehearsed for us in Book IV:

> Knowledge forbidd'n?
> Suspicious, reasonless. Why should thir Lord
> Envy them that?
> (IV. 515–17)

> is Knowledge so despis'd?
> Or envy, or what reserve forbids to taste?
> (V. 60–61)

And will be heard again in IX:

> What can your knowledge hurt him, or this Tree
> Impart against his will if all be his?
> Or is it envy?
>
> (IX. 727–9)

The temptation builds slowly, heightening the reader's anticipation of the climax. At the crucial moment, a sensory lure ('Even to my mouth of that same fruit held part / Which he had pluck't') is added to the rhetoric. Eve describes the effect on her physiological processes and on her will

> the pleasant savory smell
> So quick'n'd appetite, that I, methought,
> Could not but taste. Forthwith ...
>
> (v. 84–86)

Here the interpretative choice is offered in small. 'Methought' and 'Could not but taste' suggest imminent consent, but not consent itself. (I felt as if I had to do it.) One expects 'Forthwith' ('immediately after which' or simply 'then') to be followed by 'I reached' or 'I ate' or even 'I decided to eat.' Instead we read

> Forthwith up to the Clouds
> With him I flew.

We have missed the deed itself and passed to its effects, the literal illusion foreshadowing the metaphorical reality: 'They swim in mirth, and fancy that they feel / Divinity within them breeding wings / Wherewith to scorn the Earth' (IX. 1009–11). How are we to account for this omission? The simplest explanation consonant with the evidence is one which does credit to Eve and to her virtuous mind. Satan is unable to make Eve go through the motions of disobedience, even in her fancy, just as hypnotic suggestion cannot induce actions contrary to one's moral code. The irrevocable gesture is not reported because it does not happen. Thus Adam: 'Which gives me hope / That what in sleep thou didst abhor to dream, / Waking thou never wilt consent to do' (119–21). But some readers, intent on the Fall and on analogies which reflect 'the subconscious desires and longings' of the dreamer,[20] will hear only the irony in Adam's hope, and will assume that Eve has eaten, perhaps in the interval between 'could not but taste' and 'Forthwith', and will assume also, that, because she has, she will again, inevitably.

This interpretation of the dream, implying as it does Satan's success and Eve's involuntary compliance, is challenged at once by her disclaimer: 'but O how glad I wak'd / To find this but a dream' (92–93), which Wayne Shumaker cites as proof of 'the innocence of her will'.[21] Eve's innocence, real and technical, is even more strongly insisted on by Adam, who, with the authority displayed by the epic voice on other occasions, moves to promulgate official doctrine. (Again Milton has allowed us the latitude of speculation, and so induced a train of thought whose wrongness can now be more forcefully exposed.) Evil is present, he acknowledges, but its source can in no way be Eve: 'in thee can harbor none / Created pure' (98–99). And what of an Eve whose subconscious has been violated without her knowing it, against her will? Adam's answer is simply 'impossible I':

> Evil into the mind of God or Man
> May come and go, so unapprov'd, and leave
> No spot or blame behind.
> (117–19)

Eve could not now be the repository of evil unless her conscious will has wished it so; since her will is otherwise inclined ('O how glad'), she remains untouched (startled, not astounded) by her experience. Moreover the fact of the assault does not reflect on her firmness; rather her resistance, like the resistance of the Lady in *Comus*, affirms dramatically a basic tenet of Milton's moral philosophy:

> Virtue may be assail'd but never hurt,
> Surpris'd by unjust force but not enthrall'd,
> Yea, even that which mischief meant most harm
> Shall in the happy trial prove most glory.
> But evil on itself shall back recoil.
> (589–93)

(So Satan recoils at the touch of Ithuriel's spear, returning to 'his own shape', when he is discovered in the happy couple's bower.) One critic, describes the dream as 'a wedge for separating Eve from Adam by returning her to her mirror state',[22] but if the incident is considered apart from the Fall (as it should be), the opposite seems to be true. The fact of the dream has afforded Adam and Eve an opportunity to exercise their joint responsibilities in the manner God ordained for them. Disturbed by something she does not understand, Eve at once seeks guidance and counsel from Adam, who responds to her need with his superior wisdom.[23] The result is the strengthening of the hierarchical relationship which is the basis of their happiness and the dispelling of the anxiety occasioned by the intrusion of an alien influence. The comment of the epic voice is unequivocal:

So all was clear'd, and to the Field they haste.
(136)

Of the two invitations (to worship and to be worshipped) Eve has accepted Adam's.

The alternative reading, in which the dream is a 'portal of temptation', opened by 'some pre-existing sympathy' and leading inexorably to the Fall,[24] rests primarily on the detailed correspondences between the two passages in V and IX. Yet, reasoning from the same details, one can see, with Arthur Barker, how the incident, 'far from foreboding the Fall ... stands in the sharpest ... contrast [to] it',[25] just as Narcissus' behaviour, properly viewed, stands in contrast to Eve's. Whereas in Book IX Eve will linger at the tree, allowing Satan's logic a too easy entrance, here, even in sleep, she hears him with horror, escaping gladly to Adam's better guidance. Presumably on some other occasion, when she is not a captive audience, her rejection of the same appeal will be even more emphatic. (One more area has been removed in which virtue can be even surprised.) 'Knowing already the outcome of the story,' asserts Mrs. Bell, 'we cannot believe' Adam when he 'tells her soothingly that "evil into the mind of God or Man / May come and go."'[26] But if we do believe him, as Milton clearly intends us to, our foreknowledge points in quite another direction 'to ... the fact that the Fall is, as to right action, a parodic obliquity and anomaly.'[27] That is, the response of Adam and Eve to this situation militates against the *inevitability* (not the fact) of their later failure. As always, the pattern the details fall into is determined by the reader, who can either labour to bring the poetic moment into line with the larger perspective, or reverse the priorities by bending the poem's moral structure to fit a conclusion drawn too hastily from a local context. Ultimately the choice is between experience, the mould of the perceiving mind, and revelation, a choice mirrored here in the alternatives of believing or disbelieving Adam, and in the further obligation, if we decide to believe him, of understanding what his statement tells us about the Fall.

The episode is meant to show what Adam and Eve are capable of doing, rather than what they must inevitably do. The reader who makes the dream a cause or even a prediction of the Fall compromises prelapsarian freedom, and renders himself incapable of understanding what the loss of that freedom involves. Innocence, Raphael tells Adam and Eve, far from being static, includes large possibilities for growth as well as the possibility of declining to grow. By continuing to obey and by maturing in wisdom, as Eve matures when she recognizes Adam's superior fairness, they may ascend 'in tract of time' from the perfection of Paradise to a higher perfection;[28] and while they continue to respond to their opportunities as we see them responding here, affirming the hierarchy they were created in and labouring to do God's will, the Fall is impossible. The small crises of the middle books have been defended misleadingly as an instance of 'necessary faking' in order to avoid too abrupt a transition from innocence to sin.[29] The abruptness of the falling away, in relation to the movement of the narrative before that time, is what Milton wishes to emphasize; and he leaves us to work out the implications of these domestic adventures in the hope that we will use them to counterpoint, not circumscribe, the fatal act. The difficulty and the temptation (for us) reside in our foreknowledge, which is a liability if we ask of every word or gesture, how does this assure the Fall, and an asset if we ask instead, given the freedom of the Fall, what does this mean? Foreknowledge, like innocence, is a gift whose rewards (or hazards) are commensurate with the degree of responsibility exercised towards it. Thus if we read properly and refuse to rest in superficial resemblances, the Fall is continually thrown into brilliant relief as an incomprehensible phenomenon; otherwise we comprehend it, and by comprehending, deny it.

The tension between a responsible reading and one which results from carelessly inferring backwards from the event is particularly noticeable and significant when Adam describes his reaction to Eve:

> here passion first I felt,
> Commotion strange, in all enjoyments else

> Superior and unmov'd, here only weak
> Against the charm of Beauty's powerful glance.
> Or Nature fail'd in mee, and left some part
> Not proof enough such Object to sustain,
> Or from my side subducting, took perhaps
> More than enough; at least on her bestow'd
> Too much of Ornament, in outward show
> Elaborate, of inward less exact.
> For well I understand in the prime end
> Of Nature her th' inferior, in the mind
> And inward Faculties, which most excell
> In outward also her resembling less
> His Image who made both, and less expressing
> The character of that Dominion giv'n
> O'er other Creatures; yet when I approach
> Her loveliness, so absolute she seems
> And in herself complete, so well to know
> Her own, that what she wills to do or say,
> Seems wisest, virtuousest, discreetest, best;
> All higher knowledge in her presence falls
> Degraded.
> (VIII. 530–52)

Again we see, or should see, the unfallen consciousness rising to the challenge of its environment. Earlier Adam had asked in his ignorance, 'What meant that caution join'd, *if ye be found / Obedient*? Can we want obedience then / To him or possibly his love desert?' (V. 513–15) Now, in the light of what Raphael has told him ('That thou art happy, owe to God; / That thou continu'st such, owe to thyself'), he is able to pinpoint the area of danger ('*here* passion first I felt') and relate it to his obligations and to his answering capabilities. He admits 'strange commotions', as Eve admits her disturbing night phantasms, but, like her, he keeps his balance (startled not astounded) and retains his hold on the truth of things as he knows them to be ('For well I understand'). Higher knowledge has *not* fallen degraded in Eve's presence, and, because the possibility has been noted, it is less likely to fall in the future. The delicacy (not frailty) of Adam's understanding is mirrored in the word 'seems', a verbal extension of his will through which he controls the illusion of Eve's superiority by insisting on its status as illusion.

('Seems' is the equivalent of Eve's 'O how glad I wak'd / To find this but a dream'.) The parallelism of the two experiences extends to the eagerness in each case to consult with higher intelligences, Eve with Adam, Adam with Raphael, who, in turn, receives his information from God. Thus the entire sequence, from the first words Adam speaks in Book IV ('needs must the Power / That made us ... / Be infinitely good') to the sociable angel's departing warning at the close of Book VIII ('stand fast; to stand or fall / Free in thine own Arbitrement it lies') is an image of the harmonious co-operation possible between creatures of differing capacities who are united in their desire to understand and be faithful to the will of God.

The misgivings the captious reader may have are represented by Raphael, who, struggling as we are with the burden of foreknowledge, reacts against a future he cannot hold back and does less than justice to Adam's 'seems'. 'In loving thou dost well, in passion not', he warns. God did not intend you to be 'sunk in carnal pleasure, for which cause / Among the Beasts no Mate for thee was found.' 'Half abash't', largely, I think, because he has failed to make himself clear to someone he is anxious to please, Adam replies with new care, describing in analytical fashion the right working of his faculties:

(1) Eve's beauty, of form ('her outside ... so fair') and manner ('those graceful acts, / Those thousand decencies that daily flow / From all her words and actions'), is admired as the visible sign of an inner probity; her words and actions 'declare unfeign'd / Union of Mind, or in us both one Soul' (603–4).

(2) Even so, his consciousness of her worth does not make him her captive, because he retains his powers of judgment:

> Yet these subject not; I to thee disclose
> What inward thence I feel, not therefore foil'd,
> Who meet with various objects, from the sense
> Variously representing.
> (607–10)

(3) And he concludes by declaring his awareness of the priorities one must follow if reason is to remain right:

> still free
> Approve the best, and follow what I approve.
> (610–11)

Love (following) waits on the discernment of the best by the reason (approving) and a commitment to this order makes one free. This is the concept of love which is to be applied to the crisis of the poem, and it is delivered crisply and authoritatively here by Adam himself.

Had these words been spoken earlier, they would have been accepted as a true indication of Adam's state of mind. But here in Book VIII, shortly (in poem time) before he is said to be fondly overcome with female charm, the reader may be tempted (literally) to reason as Arnold Stein does:

> That statement, preceding so briefly the events of the following morning and noon, cannot be a satisfactory reflection of unfallen knowledge ... from the event and our consequent perspective Adam is already undergoing the conflict of temptation.
>
> (*Answerable Style*, p. 99.)

Because we know Adam will soon fall, the argument goes, he could not now be as firm as he seems to be; already corruption has occurred. This is an example of the blind alleys foreknowledge can lead us into if we use it illegitimately to determine the significance of present actions which, with 'bad recompense', then become the cause of what is foreknown. Rushing to meet 'our consequent perspective', Stein slips past the paradox Milton is at pains to impress on us at this conspicuously late stage—Adam is firm, yet Adam falls—and substitutes for it an intelligible sequence of events. Immediately, the uniqueness of the Fall as an action unrelated to its antecedents is obscured, and the focus of temptation is transferred from the will to a temporal process. (The implication that the Fall must have antecedents is a denial of the freedom of the will. Watching Eve leave Adam's side in Book IX Stein comments, 'The eating of the apple is as good as done', thereby assuming, incorrectly, that neither of them can reverse the process their separation has set in motion.)[30] The subversiveness of this reading, which can hardly be avoided as a possibility, is apparent when one sees the case of reasoning backward from it to the occasions when Adam feels the weakness he confesses, and backward still further from those occasions to the creation of that weakness (the creation of Eve) and finally to God, who becomes the prime mover in a line of cause and effect which ends in Adam's yielding. (Stein would certainly not follow his analysis to this conclusion.) If the culpability of the sinners is to be maintained as a point of belief, and understood in the framework of the poem's legalistic theology, the status of the Fall as an unforced and wholly free act must be preserved, although the effort required to isolate it from the circumstances surrounding it becomes greater as Book IX draws nearer. (The tendency of the reader to pre-date the corruption of the fallen pair is seen in another form in his infection of their language; and there is a corresponding pressure to let in fallen meanings as the crisis approaches.) The effort must be made, however, if the reader is to have a meaningful perspective on what does occur. In the context of the trial the poem represents for him, the penalty for not making it is failure.

III. THE CONSEQUENCES

One can see from this how cumulative are the effects of the interpretative choices offered by the scenes this chapter examines. Accept the Narcissus parallel in a superficial way and Eve's dream is almost certain to receive a Freudian reading. Decide that Adam dismisses the presence of evil too easily in Book V and you are halfway to deciding that he is similarly insensitive to the danger of his feelings for Eve in Book VIII. Soon Adam and Eve become the passive victims of Fate, put upon children of destiny, enmeshed, in Watkins' words, 'in an archetypal net of circumstance and mixed motivation'. They need not even be present to be further entangled. When Satan deceives Uriel, 'The sharpest sighted Spirit of all in Heav'n', who is beguiled we are told because 'neither Man nor Angel can discern / Hypocrisy', the reader is invited to ask himself if Eve, in an analogous situation, should be expected to be more discerning than one of God's eyes. The reader who has answered the question (in the negative) before he asks it will have forged another link in the chain which leads Eve to the tree. He may even suppose that Satan's entrance into Paradise, permitted by God in the incompetent persons of Uriel and Gabriel, is decisive. Yet only an instant's reflection serves to discredit the parallel and to illuminate the conditions of Eve's temptation by emphasizing the differences between the two situations. Hypocrisy is not a problem for Eve since she need only recall what God has said in response to any tempter no matter what his appearance. Uriel's failure is excusable, because he is by nature incapable of piercing Satan's disguise; in fact, his virtue works to maximize the probability of his deception. But Eve's failure is a failure of the will, inexcusable because the sufficiency of her will is not affected by the ability of an enemy to appear other than he is. Consequently Satan's presence in the garden does not in any sense assure the outcome. Again the scene is constructed in layers; on the surface one comes upon meanings which challenge the poem's overriding moral; but a slight shift of perspective and the challenge is met by the discovery of deeper and truer meanings which send us back in a new way to the truths God and Milton have proclaimed. The layer any reader reaches depends on the strength of his will and on the quality of his dedication. One may either rest in the deadening implications of the letter or penetrate to the life of the spirit.

'The great events in *Paradise Lost*', Northrop Frye has said, 'should be read ... as a discontinuous series of crises, in each of which ... the important factor is not the consequences of previous actions, but the confrontation, across a vast apocalyptic gulf', with the source of deliverance.'[31] The reader must not only see this, he must continually affirm it by refusing at every point to accede to any suggestion which impairs the freedom of such confrontations. The strain is considerable, since the basis of all his inferences is a knowledge of what is to come, and, as we have seen, that knowledge can either be well used or it can be twisted into an indictment of God. The narrator, who is also a reader, feels the strain as well as we do and we occasionally hear him labouring under it. Watching Satan light on Mt. Niphates, he cries 'O for that warning voice, which he who saw / Th' *Apocalypse*, heard cry in Heav'n aloud, / ... that now, / While time was, our first Parents had been warn'd / The coming of thir secret foe, and scap'd' (IV. 1–2, 5–7). The assumption is of a causal relationship between Satan's presence in Paradise and the Fall, and of a corresponding relationship between the availability of a warning voice and the hope of escape. But the narrator corrects himself by adding a qualification, 'Haply so scap'd', *perhaps* they would have escaped, admitting in effect that warning or no warning, with or without Satan, escape still depends on the exercise of their wills. His 'vain speculation' is an involuntary expression of his concern and sorrow, understandable, but irrelevant with respect to the point of doctrine (the freedom of the unfallen will) he accepts intellectually, and he draws back from it as we must draw back from it. Later, when Eve, 'like a Wood-Nymph light', moves off into the groves, alone, the narrator's empathy again threatens his self-control, but only for a moment:

> O much deceiv'd, much failing, hapless *Eve*,
> Of thy presum'd return! event perverse!
> Thou never from that hour in Paradise
> Found'st either sweet repast, or sound repose;
> Such ambush hid among sweet Flow'rs and Shades
> Waited with hellish rancor imminent
> To intercept thy way, or send thee back
> Despoil'd of Innocence, of Faith, of Bliss.
> For now, and since first break of dawn the Fiend,
> Mere Serpent in appearance, forth was come.
>
> (IX. 404–13)

Ricks describes perfectly the effect of the 'hesitating syntax': 'At first, one takes "deceav'd" and "failing" as absolute in their application to Eve—the poet's imagination is absorbing the full bitterness of the imminent Fall. But then the next line—"Of thy presum'd return I"—declares that she is *deceived* in the one present circumstance: her presumed return.' But his conclusion seems to me to be wrong:

> And the hesitation, as to whether 'deceav'd' and 'failing' are absolute or particular, is resolved here by our realizing that there are not in fact two paths at all, but only one. For Eve to be wrong about anything (even that she would soon be back) is for her to be wrong about everything. Before the Fall, the distinction of absolute or particular failing does not exist.
>
> (*Milton's Grand Style*, p. 97)

But the lines in question are making just that distinction. Eve's failing here is like Uriel's in Book III, innocent, and in relation to the Fall, oblique. The epic voice leaps ahead (with every reader) to what he knows *will* happen, not to what *must* happen. For Eve in the present the 'event perverse' is the event she can still prevent; this event (her leaving) is perverse only for the narrator who, yielding for an instant to the pressures generated by the narrative, imagines a necessary connection between actions which are only contiguous in time. The verse illuminates the path of error, but bars access to it, insisting even now that disaster could be avoided. When the epic voice cries, in anticipation, 'Thou never from that hour in Paradise', the reader involuntarily completes the thought with 'knew innocence' or something equally final. 'Found'st ... sweet repast' is dramatically disappointing, but morally bracing, since it effectively checks a precipitous rush toward an encounter that will come all too soon. 'Despoiled of Innocence, of Faith, of Bliss' seems absolute and present in isolation, but in context, it is controlled by the disjunctive 'or' and thus has the status of one possibility among other possibilities, including perseverance and the non-loss of innocence. The past participle 'despoil'd' is a fact held in potential despite the teasing availability of 'for now' which applies only to the coming forth of Satan. Some two hundred lines later as she contemplates the forbidden tree and considers the serpent's arguments Eve is 'yet sinless' (659), the distance between her and sin measured, as always, by the strength of her will, which is, as always, sufficient; just as the reader's will is sufficient to his task, which is to keep in mind, always, her sufficiency.

This pattern, in which the reader is presented with a series of interpretative puzzles whose solution either contributes to or undermines his understanding of the poems great issues, spans seven books. The boundary lines are God's first speech in III and Adam's final admonition to Eve in IX. (Significantly, Eve has been urging the half-truths and sophistries with which the reader has been tempted; she is, at this point, the spokesman for his subversive self, and Adam is the voice of his erected wit.)[32] These utterances share a method and a purpose. The method is logical definition, reflected stylistically in the predominance of a schematic rhetoric, and the purpose is to establish, with precision and conciseness, the capabilities and limitations of Edenic virtue (innocence). Addressing himself to the inferior intelligence of Eve and anxious to make his point unmistakable, Adam lingers longer over his argument than God does:

> his creating hand
> Nothing imperfet or deficient left
> Of all that he Created, much less Man,
> Or aught that might his happy State secure,
> Secure from outward force: within himself
> The danger lies, yet lies within his power.

> Against his will he can receive no harm.
> But God left free the Will ...
> Firm we subsist, yet possible to swerve.
> (343–51, 359)

The important distinction is made in the play on the word 'secure'. For a moment 'his happy state secure' is read as a self-contained unit asserting the *absolute* security of man's position in Paradise. (This would be true whether we take 'secure' as an adjective—'or aught that might his happy state which is secure ...'—or as a verb—'or aught that might his happy state keep safe'.) But the repetition of 'secure' with the addition of 'from outward force' qualifies the absoluteness of their security by delimiting it (secure from outward force, but vulnerable to ...) and the qualification is immediately given body in 'within himself / The danger lies'. The first within ('within himself') points to the location of the danger, and the second within ('yet lies within') refuses to locate it—physically. 'Withinness' becomes an area of spiritual dimension, non-spatial and boundless, defensible even though it is indeterminate. ('Lies' also participates in this concept.) Security for Adam and Eve is a form of anxiety; it is a state not without care, and therefore, strictly speaking, insecure. In the confines of the figure ('antanaclasis' or the 'rebound') 'secure' breaks free of its literalness to take on the flexibility of a paradox, 'secure, but not secure, yet secure as long as ...'. While they do not enjoy the false security of high walls (their walls are high, but not high enough) or effectively deployed sentries, they do enjoy the true security of a virtuous mind. 'Against his will he can receive no harm' is a conclusion that springs proven from the distinctions made in the preceding lines. The flexibility of the will is then emphasized—'But God left free the Will'—before a reformulation of the original statement is put forward: 'Firm we subsist, yet possible to swerve'.

The speech of thirty-five lines is essentially an expansion of God's 'Sufficient to have stood, though free to fall'. Properly interpreted, the intervening scenes

(1) give body to God's aphorism by dramatizing the delicate balance between the sufficiency to stand and the freedom to fall, and

(2) underline the incomprehensibility of the event.

Carelessly (subversively) interpreted, they

> (1) contribute to the confusion of the ability to fall with the certainty of falling, and
> (2) circumscribe the Fall in a network of circumstance.

In one set of readings, the complementary delicacy and strength of innocence are emphasized, and the responsibility of the unfallen pair is insisted upon; in the other, the reader assents to various oversimplifications which support the version of the story he would prefer to believe in. These oversimplifications are reflections of a desire to cheat the poem's morality, and Milton evokes them so that they can (hopefully) be exorcised. This is the most subtle of the forms the poet's 'good temptation' takes and perhaps the most 'to be desired', because by it the reader is forced to acknowledge a tendency of mind of which he may have been (consciously) unaware, and which, undetected and unjudged, could have done him irreparable harm. The temptation is baited with self-love. By the end of Book III, Satan is no longer sufficiently attractive to serve as a recipient of the reader's misguided sympathy, and he is replaced by Adam and Eve, and thus by the reader himself. For, by finding a way to transfer the responsibility for his first parents' sin to a substitute villain (Satan) or a 'natural' process (fate, circumstances), the reader in effect disclaims responsibility for the sins he himself commits; their 'technical' innocence becomes his, as does their subsequent assertion of a guilty God ('thy terms too hard').

The quality of the reader's response to these smaller actions (the deception of Uriel, the incident at the pool, Eve's dream, Adam's confession of weakness, the morning quarrel) affects his response to the Fall itself, which will either be seen in its proper light as a contrast to true virtue and right action, or misinterpreted as a necessary, and perhaps desirable, consequence of the universe's structure. Waldock observes, 'There was no way for Milton of making the transition from sinlessness to sin perfectly intelligible' (*Paradise Lost and its Critics*, p. 61). The unintelligibility, and hence the freedom, of the transition is Milton's thesis. Making it intelligible, and hence excusable, either by compromising the sufficiency of the will or by forging a chain of causality, is the reader's temptation. The seat of temptation is the reason, which, in the service of self-love, begets arguments in accord with the inclination of the affections (reason plays a flatterer's role, not unlike rhetoric's); but temptation can be resisted if the reason is directed to police itself by exposing the speciousness of its own inventions. The path taken is determined, as always, by the will. For the reader too, the danger lies within, 'yet lies within his power. / Against his, will he can receive no harm.'

Notes

1. *A Preface to Paradise Lost* (Oxford, 1942), pp. 69–70.
2. *Paradise Lost as 'Myth'*, p. 183.
3. Actually the opposite is true: if they could not fall they could not stand; that is, they would not be doing the standing, consciously and wilfully. The ability not to fall depends on the ability to fall; free will is a meaningless concept unless the possibility of wrong choice exists.
4. Milton (London, 1957), p. 181.
5. Daniel Dyke, *The Mystery of Selfe-Deceiving* (1615), pp. 355, 7. See Miller and Johnson, *The Puritans* (rev. edn., 1963), i.284: 'A large quantity of Puritan sermons were devoted ... to exposing not merely the conscious duplicity of evil men, but the abysmal tricks which the subconscious can play upon the best of men.'
6. *The Mystery of Self-Deceiving*, p. 138.
7. 'Thus did Adam, when he said in defence of his owne eating, the *woman* thou *gavest me, she gave me it*, closely taxing God himselfe, as if hee should have said, unlesse thou hadst given mee this companion, I had not eaten ... God that hateth, forbiddeth, threateneth, punisheth sinne, can he possibly, tempt unto sinne? Yea, but thou sayest hee decreed my sinne, for nothing comes to passe without his will. The *second* causes move not, unlesse they bee moved by the *first*. I answer the first cause is not the cause of the errour that is in the motion of the *second*, though it be the cause of the *motion*. As in the wheeles of a clocke, the principall wheele, with its motion, runnes about the lower, yet if there be any errour in the motion of the lower, it is no cause at all thereof. Now, sinne is not properly any motion, but an *errour* in the motion of thy heart. Gods will being the first cause, is the cause of thy hearts motion ... but if there be any sinne, any errour in the motion, thine owne will is the cause thereof. For all that God hath to doe about it, is his *voluntary permission* whereby he, withdrawing his grace from thee, leaveth thee to thy selfe, as not beeing bounde unto thee. He doth

not infuse, or instill into thy minde any wicked motions, as doth *Sathan*. Hee onely setteth the baite, or the net, and doth not refraine thy concupiscence from carrying thee to it: for he owes thee no such service: but he doth not take poles, as Sathan doeth, and drive thee violently into the net. And yet if *Sathan's temptation* could not excuse Adam, how much lesse then *Gods desertion*' (152–3). See also Richard Baxter, *The arrogancy of Reason* (1655), p. 65, where the same quibble is considered and rejected: 'Nor is it any deifying of the Creatures will to say it is such a self-determining principle, and so far a first cause, while it had the power of self-determination from God, and so absolutely is no first cause! Obviously, the various ways of absolving oneself of guilt were much discussed; and this increases the likelihood that Milton would have expected his readers to recognize their objections to the doctrine of free will for what they are, the unlawful urgings of the carnal reason. Another of the 'scapegoats' Dyke disallows is Satan, in a passage that has relevance for *Paradise Lost*: 'The Divell cannot prevaile against us, but by the helpe of our owne corruption. He might strike fire long enough, ere there would be any burning, did not wee finde him tinder' (p. 151).

8. *Reason of Church Government, Complete Prose Works*, i.817.
9. Thomas Watson, *Christian Soldier*, p. 48.
10. The possibility of being unconsciously subversive is discussed by Milton in the *Christian Doctrine* (*The Works of John Milton*, xiv. 101, 103): 'That the fall of man was not necessary is admitted on all sides; but if such, nevertheless, was the nature of the divine decree, that his fall became really inevitable, *both which opinions, however contradictory, are sometimes held by the same persons*, then the restoration of man, after he had lapsed of necessity, became no longer a matter of grace on the part of God, but of simple justice! By keeping the two points of belief (the Fall was not necessary, the decree made it inevitable) in separate compartments, the mind entertains blasphemy on a subconscious level, while being outwardly orthodox. Milton makes this manoeuvre impossible by forcing an awareness of the contradictions involved in holding these and like opinions, much as the process of dialectic forces awareness (and choice) upon the respondent: 'The respondent now is confronted with an alternative and a choice. Either he erred in making the initial and succeeding agreements leading to this evident, albeit discomfiting, consequence; or his previous opinions were without foundation. If he decides that he erred in his initial *doxa* or somewhere along the way, he is obligated to indicate at what point and why. If he

concludes that he was ill-advised in making concessions to begin with, he is convicted of subordinating truth to prudential interests. If he determines, willy-nilly, to reaffirm his original proposition, he must at least concede that he is on record for holding contrary or contradictory judgments. Eventually he may be led to square himself with himself. Meanwhile, like Alcibiades in the *Symposium*, the man will be self-convicted until he is self-convinced (216c).' Robert Cushman, *Therapeia* (Chapel Hill, 1958), p. 235.

11. Cf. III. 128–31: 'they themselves ordain'd thir fall / The first sort by thir own suggestion fell, / Self-tempted, self deprav'd: Man falls deceiv'd / By th' other first: Man therefore shall find grace'. The implication in the syntax is that grace is due man because his error is someone else's responsibility: Man *therefore* shall find grace. But this is deliberate teasing, if not on God's part, then on Milton's. The 'therefore' is not logical, but arbitrary; Satan's presence in the garden is not really an extenuating circumstance; God merely chooses to make it the basis of an action that proceeds solely from his goodwill. The urgings of the Devil may render obedience difficult (or perhaps make it easier) but never impossible. God points the moral beforehand, 'Sufficient to have stood, though free to fall' (99), a line that will pursue us into Book IX. Man does ordain his own fall, and we always know it to be so, but a decoy like 'therefore' is nevertheless able to make us go against our knowledge, for a moment; we want very much to read 'deserve' instead of 'find' grace, and do so until the word 'mercy' reminds us that grace is gratuitous, cannot be earned and certainly not deserved: 'But Mercy first and last shall brightest shine'. The experience of this passage and others like it can be compared to the experience of making a typing error. Even as the finger presses the wrong key, something in the mind flashes a warning signal; but the reflexes are too slow, a mistake is made, and one simultaneously participates in and analyses a failure in co-ordination.

12. As readers of *Paradise Lost*, we are in a curious position, analogous to that proposed by one critic for the narrator of Chaucer's *Troilus and Criseide*: 'By the beginning of Book IV ... the narrator's love for Criseide has become such that when he finds himself forced to face the issue of her perfidy he comes close to denying the truth of his old books.... It is a strange historian who becomes so emotionally involved with the personages of his history that he is willing to impugn the reliability of the sources upon which his whole knowledge of those personages presumably depends.' (E. T. Donaldson, *Chaucer's Poetry: in*

Mythology for the Modern Reader, New York, 1958, p. 967.) This is true to some extent of Milton's narrator, but truer still of his reader who becomes 'emotionally involved' with the originals of himself. Despite certain knowledge of the history and a unique commitment to its source (the sacred text) he finds himself increasingly eager to deny the fact of the Fall and thus avoid the issue of his own perfidy, either by ascribing it to a natural and therefore innocent depravity or by fixing the blame on some other agent. The latter is the more attractive alternative, since it seems to preserve the free will of the victims, at least superficially; actually there is no difference at all between believing that Adam and Eve could not help but fall or believing that their fall was caused by someone else, and in the end this kind of reasoning inevitably returns to God.

13. *Criticism of Paradise Lost*, p. 102; *The Club of Hercules*, p. 74.
14. *The Muse's Method*, p. 98.
15. Harding, loc. cit.
16. Waldock, op. cit., p. 61.
17. Newton (*Paradise Lost*, 1749) notes that Addison asks 'sarcastically enough [*Spectator*, vol. 5, No. 325.] whether some moral is not couch'd under this place, where the poet lets us know, that the first woman immediately after her creation ran to a looking-glass, and became so enamour'd of her own face, that she had never removed to view any of the other works of nature, had not she been led off to a man.' Newton's defence of Eve sets the pattern for all subsequent defences: 'This account that Eve gives of her coming to a lake, and there falling in love with her own image ... is much more probable and *natural* as well as more delicate and beautiful, than the famous story of Narcissus in Ovid, from which our author manifestly took the hint, and has expertly imitated some passages, but has avoided all his puerilities ... as the reader may observe by comparing them both together' (emphasis mine).
18. *The Return of Eden*, p. 75.
19. The distinction between 'startle' and 'astound' is the basis of the definition of virtue offered in the masque. Milton conceives of virtue as a state of inner composure, a moral readiness that cannot be shaken, even by something totally unexpected. The virtuous mind may be surprised (startled) at a possibility hitherto unknown (as Adam will be surprised to discover that he can disobey) without losing its balance; it will absorb and assimilate new facts and situations, not disintegrate before them. On the other hand, a mind that is astounded has allowed

the weight of external pressures to paralyse and rout it; it has become the plaything of circumstances instead of their master. The fallen angels are 'astounded' or stupefied by their situation in Hell (I. 281).

20. Harding, op. cit., p. 83.

21. 'The Fallacy of the Fall in *Paradise Lost*', *PMLA*, lxx (1955), 1186.

22. Stein, *Answerable Style*, p. 93.

23. When we first meet Eve she is receiving instruction from Adam's lips; later she is said to prefer his teaching to the angel Raphael's (VIII. 50–57). In Book IX, Eve will again seek Adam's approval or counsel, and for the first time he handles the situation badly with what results we know (the separation, not the Fall). Appropriately, the reconciliation scene in Book X is a reestablishment of the old relationship.

24. Millicent Bell, 'The Fallacy of the Fall in *Paradise Lost*', *PMLA*, lxviii (1953), 871; E. M. W. Tillyard, *Studies in Milton* (London, 1951), p. 11.

25. 'Structural and Doctrinal Patterns in Milton's Later Poems', in *Essays in English Literature From the Renaissance to the Victorian Age presented to A. S. P. Woodhouse*, ed. Maclure and Watt (Toronto, 1964.), p. 190.

26. Loc. cit.

27. Barker, loc. cit.

28. The term 'perfection' has been the cause of some confusion. Mrs. Bell argues, 'the mind can not accept the fact that perfection was capable of corruption without denying the absoluteness of perfection' (op. cit., p. 863). But if Adam and Eve are perfect, they are perfect with respect to their species, not absolutely perfect. Absolute perfection belongs to God; human perfection demands that man be able (free) to make mistakes. One must distinguish between flaws and limitations; man's limitations (his distance from absolute perfection) are the basis of his dignity and therefore one aspect of his perfection. See Summers, *The Muse's Method*, p. 149: 'We have already noted some of the ways in which the poem presents perfection as moving rather than static, as relative rather than absolute. Adam and Eve are created perfect for their place (although the place may change); they are endowed with the possession or the possibility of perfect fulfilment in time, of perfect happiness and joy and the perfection of all the knowledge of which they are capable in their state; and they are also endowed with the ability to doubt or

distrust or forget their happiness and perfection, the ability to deny and to destroy it all.'

29. 'In Book Four of *Paradise Lost* Milton pictured his state of innocence.... But he could not possibly have conducted his account of the Fall with that picture for sole starting point; the effect would have been sudden and violent and would have carried no conviction.... Instead he resorts to some faking; perfectly legitimate in a Poem, yet faking nevertheless. He anticipates the Fall by attributing to Eve and Adam feelings which though nominally felt in the state of innocence are actually not compatible with it.' (Tillyard, *Studies in Milton*, pp. 10–11.) 'Theologically and symbolically he [Adam] is innocent until he has to act. But Milton could not construct his fiction entirely from that perspective; he needed a scope of action sufficient for conflict and he needed both direct and symbolic action that could borrow meaning, as it were, by anticipating human experience after the Fall.' (Stein, *Answerable Style*, p. 99.) 'As a theologian, Milton was compelled to maintain a spotless innocence in Adam and Eve until that precise moment when Eve actually eats the Fruit. As a poet, he was compelled to anticipate the Fall by implying in both our first parents not only a predisposition to sin but the specific frailty out of which the sin could grow.... These two aims are clearly incompatible.... To accomplish by artifice what could not be accomplished in fact, Milton sought to implant in the minds of his readers a secret, furtive, tentative uneasiness about Adam and Eve—not so much doubts as the shadow of doubts—while simultaneously maintaining the illusion of their entire sinlessness.' (Harding, *The Club of Hercules*, pp. 68–69.) Implied in these statements is a confusion between the ability to fall and the process of actually falling. Harding's 'entire sinlessness' is equivalent to Mrs. Bell's 'absolute perfection'; They both assume the staticness of innocence. When Tillyard writes of 'feelings incompatible with the state of innocence' he is much more purist than Milton or his God. The only feeling incompatible with innocence is the I-must-eat-the-apple feeling, and even there the psychic decision to do so and the physical commission of the deed must follow before innocence is lost.

30. *Answerable Style*, p. 102. The decision to separate is unfortunate, but not fatal. Separation no more assures the Fall than staying together would *certainly* have prevented it. Adam explains to Eve that they will be 'most likely' (IX. 365) to avoid temptation if they do not separate. All actions save one are lawful in Paradise, although some are

inadvisable. No sequence of inadvisable actions (physical or mental) can overwhelm the unfallen will and determine its direction, for at any point it can disengage itself from the pressures that seek to influence it, whether they originate from the outside or from within. The free will is *absolutely* free.

31. *The Return of Eden*, pp. 102–3.

32. Eve confuses heroic virtue with prideful self-assertion when she asks, 'And what is Faith, Love, Virtue unassay'd / Alone, without exterior help sustain'd?' (335–6). She also mistakes the flexibility of the free will for imperfection: 'Let us not then suspect our happy State / Left so imperfet by the Maker wise, / As not secure so single or combin'd. / Frail is our happiness, if this be so, / And *Eden* were no *Eden* thus expos'd.' Her arguments correspond to the speculations entertained by the reader (heroism requires a dramatic situation, if they could fall, they were already in some sense fallen) and he must reject them or agree with Adam's rejection of them. The tension in the scene is a reflection of the tension within him.

LAURA LUNGER KNOPPERS

Paradise Regained
and the Politics of Martyrdom

At the later end of the year 1648 I had leave given mee to goe to london to see my Father & during my stay there at that time at Whitehall it was that I saw the Beheading of King Charles the first; He went by our door on Foot each day that hee was carry'd by water to Westminster, for hee took Barge at Garden-stayres where wee liv'd, & once hee spake to my Father & sayd Art thou alive yet! On the day of his execution, which was Tuesday, Jan. 30, I stood amongst the crowd in the street before Whitehal gate, where the scaffold was erected, and saw what was done, but was not so near as to hear any thing. The Blow I saw given, & can truly say with a sad heart; at the instant whereof, I remember wel, there was such a Grone by the Thousands then present, as I never heard before & desire I may never hear again. [PHILLIP HENRY diary][1]

The execution of Charles I followed nearly a decade of fighting in print and with arms over the nature and limits of kingship.[2] The revolutionary Independents had, with the support of the army, purged parliament and set up the Court of High Commission, which tried, condemned, and sentenced Charles. Both the trial and execution were public displays,

---

From *Modern Philology*, vol. 90, no. 2: pp. 200-219. Published by The University of Chicago Press. © 1992 by the University of Chicago. All Rights Reserved.

designed to persuade the people that Charles was being justly punished for capital offenses against then). But the groan of the crowd as the king's head was severed from his body might have warned the revolutionaries of an audience not quite so tractable or convinced as they had hoped. In its response the audience demonstrated that the effects of punishment cannot be fully controlled by the mechanisms of exemplary power. The public display of punishment, dependent upon its audience, was immediately challenged and subverted by the discourse of martyrdom. The execution was followed shortly by the publication of *Eikon Basilike*, the "King's Book," which interpreted Charles's refusal to submit to the court not as obstinacy but as constancy, and his death not as just punishment for treason but as martyrdom. The cult of royal martyrdom which the *Eikon Basilike* initiated would meet with a determined and defiant opponent in John Milton. But, paradoxically, the royal martyr would not die.

I

Despite their victory over Charles in the field, the revolutionaries struggled in the trial and execution to win the ideological battle. On January 6, 1649, the Commons accused Charles of tyranny, treason, and murder, charging that he had "a wicked designe totally to subvert the antient and fundamentall lawes and liberties of this nation. And in theire place to introduce an arbitrary and tiranicall government ... and hath prosecuted it with fire and sword, levied and maintayned a cruell warre in the land against the Parliament and kingdome."[3] The public trial of Charles I shows a transitional stage of power between what Michel Foucault has delineated as the arbitrary torture perpetrated by the ancien régime in France—a means of inducing horror and terror in the viewer—and more condign punishment which links the ideas of crime and penalty in the minds of the viewers.[4] The trial and execution were part of the dramaturgy of state, designed to convince its audience that the text of Charles's life must be read as treason, his death as "exemplary and condigne punishment." The high court appealed to the rhetoric of justice and divine providence to supplement or, more accurately, occlude the force underlying the trial. John Cook, lawyer for the prosecution, described the proceedings as "the most Comprehensive, Impartial and Glorious piece of Justice that ever was acted and Executed upon the

Theatre of England."⁵ The Court of High Commission had not only a juridical but also a moral and theological function. Shifting among various Old Testament models by which their actions could be interpreted and justified, the court fastened on the notion of bloodguilt. According to Cook, they acted for a higher court in trying and judging Charles, "whom God in his wrath gave to be a King to this nation, and will, I trust, in great love, for his notorious Prevarications and Blood guiltiness take him away from us." In a drama that is allegorical and didactic, Charles "stands now to give an account of his stewardship and to receive the good of justice, for all the evil of his injustice and cruelty."⁶

By staging the trial as a public display, the regicides strove to justify but also exposed to open challenge the legitimacy of their cause. And Charles refused to play his given role. The king acted out the part not of a penitent sinner, which would have confirmed their case, but of a constant sufferer for liberty and truth. Refusing to recognize the authority of the court, he continually exposed the force which the display of justice attempted to cover: "It is not my case alone, it is the Freedom and the Liberty of the people of England; and do you pretend what you will, I stand more for their Liberties. For if power without law may make lawes, may alter the fundamental laws of the kingdom, I do not know what subject he is in England, that can be sure of his life or any thing that he calls his own."⁷ Charles rewrites the script, recasting the regicides' justice as a power which unlawfully threatens king and subject alike. As a king betrayed and tried by his own subjects, not allowed to speak in a court claiming justice, Charles soon found a more effective paradigm by which he could sustain and explain his case—that of martyrdom and, in particular, the royal martyrdom of Christ.

The scaffold as a theater for punishment, twinned with the public trial, shows the force of law and justice inscribed in the very body of the condemned. Yet the display of the punished traitor does not produce a single meaning. As Foucault explains, there is "an ambiguity in this suffering that may signify equally well the truth of the crime or the error of the judges, the goodness or evil of the criminal, the coincidence or the divergence between the judgement of men and that of God."⁸ Ironically, the Independents themselves make Charles a martyr by trying and executing him publicly. Charles's speech and demeanor during his trial and execution, fully reported and put into circulation, have unexpected consequences. On the scaffold, as during the trial, Charles refuses to play his assigned role. No scaffold confession, acknowledging his own guilt and the justice of the state which punishes him, is forthcoming. On the contrary, Charles asserts his innocence and models himself on the royal martyr, Christ. Like Christ, he forgives his enemies: "I have forgiven all the world, and even those in particular that have been the chief causes of my death.... I pray God forgive them." Claiming to die as "the Martyr of the people," Charles looks to a crown of martyrdom: "I go from a corruptible to an incorruptible crown, where no disturbance can be, no disturbance in the world." He bravely meets the execution which follows: "After a little pause, the King stretching forth his hands, the Executioner at one blow severed his head from his body, and held it up and shewed it to the people, saying, 'Behold the head of a Traitor.'"[9] But already the theater of punishment was crumbling.

In ceremonies of public execution the main character was the crowd, whose presence and belief was required for the performance. But the audience at Charles's execution was unreliable. Philip Henry reports that the soldiers, apparently fearing a negative reaction, immediately dispersed the crowd: "There was according to Order one Troop immediately marching from-wards charing-cross to Westm[inster] & another from-wards Westm[inster] to charing cross purposely to masker the people, & to disperse & scatter them, so that I had much adoe amongst the rest to escape home without hurt."[10] The audience did not cooperate in the official spectacle but sought another meaning, another kind of tragedy. A Royalist newspaper, *Mercurius Elencticus* (Tuesday, January 30), reports that the people rushed to buy relics of the dead king. For the people Charles was a martyr; for the soldiers he was a means of making money: "When they had murdered him, such as desired to dip their handkerchiefes or other things in his blood, were admitted for moneys. Others bought peeces of board which were dy'd with his blood, for which the soldiers took of some a shilling, of others half a crowne, more or less according to the quality of the persons that sought it. But none without ready money." The soldiers continued to profit: "And after his body was coffin'd, as many as desired to see it were permitted at a certaine rate, by which meanes the soldiers got store of moneys, insomuch that one was heard to say 'I would we had two or three more such Majesties to behead, if we could but make such use of them.'"[11] The soldier's wish would be granted, although not in the form he might have imagined. Charles would indeed reappear in the ensuing cult of royal martyrdom which left the regicides and Cromwellian government with many Charleses to confront, many new majesties to behead.

II

The publication of *Eikon Basilike* immediately after Charles's execution marked a new stage in the struggle between the monarch and his foes. "Prayers and tears" would ultimately be more effective than the weapons of warfare which had failed to make good the king's cause, the discourse of martyrdom more effective than the spectacle of treason. After the Restoration, the probable coauthor (or true author) of *Eikon Basilike*, John Gauden, exulted in martial metaphor over its publication: "When it came out, just upon the King's death; Good God! What shame, rage and despite filled hys Murtherers! What comfort hys friends! How many enemyes did it convert! How many hearts did it mollify, and melt! ... What preparations it made in all men's minds for this happy restauration.... In a word, it was an army, and did vanquish more than any sword could."[12] Although much of the *Eikon Basilike* gives a detailed defense of Charles's political actions and decisions, most compelling are its rhetoric of piety and claim to a Christlike martyrdom for Charles that skillfully adapts the precedent of John Foxe's "Book of Martyrs."[13] *Eikon Basilike* impresses Charles's story with the distinctive contours of Foxe's martyrology as the king endures affliction, remains true to his conscience, and suffers the rage and malice of his enemies. But the "King's Book" also conflates Charles's sufferings with Christ's, merging the Foxean portrait of the martyr with the rich and resonant biblical and literary tradition of royal martyrdom. In so doing, *Eikon Basilike* develops a powerful discourse for idealizing Charles and stigmatizing his enemies.

Like the "Book of Martyrs," *Eikon Basilike* is self-consciously concerned with defining and portraying true martyrdom. Charles explicitly claims this status: "They knew my chiefest arms left me were those only which the ancient Christians were wont to use against their persecutors—prayers and tears. These may serve a good man's turn, if not to conquer as a soldier, yet to suffer as a martyr" (p. 47). And he denies martyrdom to his political opponents: "Some parasitic preachers have dared to call those 'martyrs' who died fighting against the me, the laws, their oaths, and the religion established. But sober Christians know that glorious title can with truth be applied only to those who sincerely preferred God's truth and their duty in all these particulars before their lives and all that was dear to them in this world" (pp. 118–19). Charles claims the martyrs' constancy, commenting: "Here I am sure to be conqueror if God will give me such a measure of constancy as to fear him more than man and to love the inward peace of my conscience before any outward tranquility" (p. 38), for, "what they [my enemies] call obstinacy, I know God accounts honest constancy" (p. 138). Charles also prays: "*Give me that measure of patience and constancy which my condition now requires*" (p. 139). Such frequent references to conscience, patience, and constancy create a compelling portrait of Charles, the martyr-king.

While the "King's Book" portrays Charles as suffering and dying for the church as well as for the more strictly political cause of monarchy, the issues are inseparable because this martyr's truth is bound even more to an internal political power struggle than are those in Foxe's massive ionic. While it would be naive to deny the political implications in Foxe's virulently anti-Catholic accounts of martyrdom, his Marian martyrs at least debate theological issues, albeit ones with political import—transubstantiation, purgatory and the penitential system (confession, indulgences, meritorious works), marriage of the clergy, and papal supremacy. *Eikon Basilike* appropriates and further politicizes the discourse of martyrdom, employing its rhetoric to interpret such specific events and points of dispute in the English civil war as "His Majesty's Calling This Last Parliament," "The Listing and Raising Armies against the King," "Their Seizing the King's Magazines, Forts, Navy, and Militia," and "The Various Events of the War: Victories and Defeats" (pp. vii–viii). But despite the increased attention to details of contemporary political events, Gauden (with Charles) is able to draw much more fully than Foxe had on the tradition of Christ as royal martyr. Foxe's own relationship to monarchy is complex if not problematic.[14] Foxe writes to support Elizabeth and the established church, to advise the queen in her destined role as true sovereign; yet the martyrdoms he most vividly and elaborately recounts are those of middle- and lower-class subjects under conformity proceedings mandated by another monarch—bloody Queen Mary. Although Foxe briefly recounts Christ's passion and crucifixion, he makes no real use of the resonant biblical and literary tradition of Christ as royal martyr. *Eikon Basilike* thus draws on and dramatically revises the Foxean tradition in its compelling portrait of the martyr-king.

Associations with Christ's sufferings, passion, and death resonate throughout the "King's Book," elevating Charles's cause and stigmatizing his political enemies as traitors. "His Majesty's Retirement from Westminster" and his refusal to comply with parliamentary demands are presented as a choice of kingly martyrdom: "I will rather choose to wear a crown of thorns with my Saviour than to exchange that of gold, which is due to me, for one of lead" (p. 28). Foregrounding his divine type, Charles implicitly compares "Raising Armies against the King" with the crucifixion of a forgiving Christ: *"when Thy wrath is appeased by my death, O remember Thy great mercies toward them and forgive them, O my Father, for they know not what they do"* (p. 46). The "Troubles in Ireland" (in which the king stood accused of fomenting a Catholic uprising) are depicted in terms of Christ's suffering on the cross: "Therefore with exquisite malice they have mixed the gall and vinegar of falsity and contempt with the cup of my affliction" (p. 63). Similarly, the "Scots Delivering the King to the English" is compared to Judas's selling of Christ: "If I am sold by them, I am only sorry they should do it and that my price should be so much above my Saviour's" (p. 137).

Finally, in the "Meditations upon Death" which conclude *Eikon Basilike*, Charles moves from justifying specific actions to constructing more fully the myth of the royal martyr by which his life and death may be interpreted. Charles refers to "those greater formalities whereby my enemies, (being more solemnly cruel) will, it may be, seek to add (as those who crucified Christ) the mockery of justice to the cruelty of malice" (p. 174). Echoing Christ's words in the garden of Gethsemane, Charles professes willingness to accept the bitter cup: *"Thou givest me leave as a man to pray that this cup may pass from me; but Thou hast taught me as a Christian by the example of Christ to add, not my Will, but Thine be done"* (p. 181). He claims continuity with Christ's martyrdom: "If I must suffer a violent death with my Saviour, it is but mortality crowned with martyrdom" (p. 179). And Charles is explicit in acknowledging that his martyrdom will be a paradoxical victory: "My next comfort is that He gives me not only the honor to imitate His example in suffering for righteousness' sake, (though obscured by the foulest charges of tyranny and injustice), but also that charity which is the noblest revenge upon and victory over, my destroyers" (p. 176). Like Foxe's martyrs whose constancy in burning at the stake astonished and amazed onlookers, and like Christ on the cross, to whom the Roman centurion pays tribute, Charles will experience death but no defeat. The regicides' apparent failure to understand the power of martyrdom is a crucial and ultimately irreparable mistake.

III

The "King's Book" brilliantly subverted the exemplary power of the state, recasting the public trial and execution of Charles as a drama of suffering and martyrdom. Gauden's colleagues responded in kind. The book initiated an outpouring of elegies and hyperbolic laments on Charles the royal martyr.[15] Focusing on his final days and his death, the martyrologies greatly elaborate the parallels with Christ's passion and crucifixion, paying little attention to details of the political struggle. Diverging from Foxe and elaborating on the *Eikon Basilike*, the martyrologies construct a full picture of Charles as a uniquely royal martyr. For the first time, Charles is given a sympathetic—even weeping—audience. The author of *An Elegie Upon the Death of Our Dread Soveraign Lord King CHARLS the MARTYR* is typical: "Com, com let's mourn; all eies, that see this *Daie*, / Melt into Showrs, and Weep your selvs awaie: / O that each Private head could yield a Flood / Of Tears, whil'st *Britain's Head* stream's out His Blood."[16] Flouting state censorship, the martyrologies poignantly link Charles with Christ in his passion and death, blackening the regicides with the powerfully resonant myth of the crucifixion.

The martyrologies recast the alleged justice of Charles's public trial and execution as a false, theatrical reenactment of Christ's trial and crucifixion. In a sermon which he would preach again eleven years later before Charles II, the bishop of Downe turns from the passion and death of Christ "to present unto you another sad tragedy, so like unto the former, that it may seem but *vetus fabula per novos histriones*, the stage onely changed, and new actors entred upon it."[17] *A Deepe Groane Fetch'd At the Funerall of that Incomparable and Glorious Monarch, Charles the First* elaborates more fully on the tragic play:

> Such was their Bedlame Rabble, and the Cry
> Of *Justice* now, 'mongst them was *Crucifie*:
> *Pilates* Consent is *Bradshawes* Sentence here;
> The *Judgement hall's* remov'd to *Westminster*.
> Hayle to the Reeden Scepture the Head, and knee
> Act o're againe that Cursed Pageantrie.[18]

In this mock trial, Charles bears a unique resemblance to Christ. The Independents become the "Bedlame Rabble," Bradshaw takes the role of

Pilate, and the trial at Westminster reenacts the "Cursed Pageantrie."

Focusing thus on the final days and hours of the king's life, elegies and sermons multiply links between the sufferings of Charles and Christ, much to the detriment of the king's accusers. *A Hand-Kirchife for Loyall Mourners* asserts,

> It is a heavy thing to think on, that he should suffer by his own Judasses. But a joyfull and glorious thing it is to think on, that he suffered so like his own Jesus, so like him in the manner, and circumstances of his sufferings being betrayed by his owne servants, arraigned before Jewes and *Pilate*, at the best, reviled, reproached, and they say spit upon by an unworthy varlet, scorned and contemned & condemned unto death: so like him in the temper of his sufferings, with so much meeknesse and fortitude, undauntedness of spirit, and submission to the will of God.[19]

A number of tracts and sermons insist that the parallels between Charles and Christ are both striking and singular. *The Scotch Souldiers Lamentation Upon the Death of the most Glorious and Illustrious Martyr, King Charles* concludes, "There have beene many Martyrs, but no Martyr-Kings that I know of but my blessed Saviour Christ Jesus, and my late gracious Soveraigne Lord King Charles."[20]

In 1660, the martyrology tracts again proliferated with the restoration of the king's son, Charles II. Royalists republished and embellished *lachrymae ecclesiasticae* whose pathos and hyperbole were much the same as those in elegies, sermons, and memorials published just after the execution eleven years earlier. But now the tragedy turns to tragicomedy, even to comedy; the king's murderers are banished from the stage and the new king installed in the leading role. Anthonie Sadler's *The Loyall Mourner, Shewing the Murdering of King Charles the First: Fore-shewing the Restoring of King Charles the Second* traces the developments of the past decade: "The King's Beheaded: and the Royall Crown's / Stript of *Monarchall* Rule: the Nobles down: / The Souldier sways the judge: the Sword, the Law: / A Lawless Sword doth all the Kingdom awe." Suddenly now the play has changed:

> the Theater's new Hung,
> A Proclamation made, the Bells are Rung,

> The King's Receiv'd, Loyalties Return'd
> All in a night, and welcome Formes Reform'd,
> Peace Crowns the Kingdom, *all* in each degree,
> Act *pleasant* parts, and play a Comedy.[21]

The triumphal return of Charles II and the punishment of those who had supported the regicide seemed to confirm the martyrdom of Charles I; the true church, afflicted under the republic, was now restored.

The publishing and republishing of the martyrologies and the *Eikon Basilike* thus had important political ramifications in Restoration England. Like Foxe's "Book of Martyrs" dedicated to Elizabeth, the martyrologies implicitly or explicitly pointed to Charles II as the true monarch about to restore the church. And also like Foxe, the martyrologies instructed and guided Charles in the manner of establishing that church. The cult of the royal martyr exonerated the Anglican clergy, blackened the Independents, and provided a text by which to interpret the display of the new, even more theatrical Restoration monarchy. Even in their political victory, the Royalists seemed to retain firm control of the powerful discourse of martyrdom.

IV

In publishing the text of Charles's trial and execution and allowing the *Eikon* and the martyrologies to escape censorship, the Independents had seriously miscalculated the effects of the public execution. Too late, the new government commissioned John Milton to answer the "King's Book." Milton's *Eikonoklastes* (1649), although primarily a point-by-point rebuttal of the *Eikon Basilike*, also recognizes the cult of royal martyrdom which the "King's Book" had fostered. Milton rebukes the preachers who "howle in thir Pulpits" after the dead Charles and he tries (futilely, in the event) to repel the rhetoric of martyrdom with a combination of scorn and reason.[22] Milton attacks the *Eikon Basilike*, first of all, by reversing the charges of stagecraft: Charles's alleged martyrdom is false theatricality dependent on a deluded and idolatrous audience.[23] The frontispiece of the *Eikon Basilike*, which depicts a kneeling Charles about to exchange his golden crown for a crown of thorns, aims, according to Milton, to "Martyr him and Saint him to befool the people" (p. 343). The "conceited portraiture" of Charles is sleight-of-hand stage work, "drawn out to the full measure of a Masking Scene, and sett there to catch fools and silly gazers" (p. 342). Such "quaint Emblems and devices begg'd from the Old Pageantry of some Twelf-nights entertainment at *Whitehall* will doe but ill to make a Saint or Martyr" (p. 343). The "King's Book" is to be rejected as false and theatrical: "Stage-work will not doe it; much less *the justness of thir Cause*" (p. 530).

And yet the people are easy prey. Milton heaps scorn not only on the royal actor but on his gullible, doting, idolatrous audience: "The People, exorbitant and excessive in all thir motions, are prone ofttimes not to a religious onely, but to a civil kinde of Idolatry in idolizing thir Kings" (p. 343). The "King's Book" shows "what a miserable, credulous, deluded thing that creature is, which is call'd the Vulgar" (p. 426). Charles will never "stirr the constancie and solid firmness of any wise Man" but will only "catch the worthles approbation of an inconstant, irrational, and Image-doting rabble" (p. 601). The people, like a "credulous and hapless herd, begott'n to servility, and inchanted with these popular institutes of Tyranny" are themselves witness to "thir own voluntary and beloved baseness" (p. 601).

Charles's claim to martyrdom, then, is false and theatrical; the people's responses to such a claim are idolatrous and deluded. Milton scornfully dismisses Charles's claim to a Christlike crown of thorns since Charles, unlike Christ, suffers for his own faults: "Many would be all one with our Saviour, whom our Saviour will not know. They who govern in those Kingdoms which they had a right to, have to our Saviours Crown of Thornes no right at all. Thornes they may find anow, of thir own gathering, and thir own twisting ... but to weare them as our Saviour wore them is not giv'n to them that suffer by thir own demerits" (pp. 417–18). According to Milton, Charles's self-promotion undermines his own cause since "Martyrs bear witness to the truth, not to themselves": "If I beare witness of my self, saith *Christ*, my witness is not true. He who writes himself *Martyr* by his own inscription, is like an ill Painter, who, by writing on the shapeless Picture which he hath drawn, is fain to tell passengers what shape it is; which els no man could imagin" (p. 575). Suffering or dying with constancy, Milton objects, does not make a martyr: "Lastly, if to die for *the testimony of his own conscience*, be anough to make him Martyr, what Heretic dying for direct blasphemie, as som have don constantly, may not boast a Martyrdom?" (p. 576).

In discounting Charles's suffering and emphasizing the truth for which genuine martyrs suffer, Milton implicitly revives the etymology of martyrdom—"witnessing." If Milton primarily focuses in *Eikonoklastes* on denying Charles the name of martyr, he also constructs his own text as a counterexample, a true martyr or witness to the truth before God and man. *Eikonoklastes* comes to counter the king's false claims to the truth, impelled by the king's "making new appeale to Truth and the World" and leaving "this Book," *Eikon Basilike*, "as the best advocat and interpreter of his own actions" so that "his Friends by publishing, dispersing, commending, and almost adoring it, seem to place therein the chiefe strength and nerves of thir cause" (p. 340). Milton will oppose the *Eikon Basilike* by "remembring them the truth of what they themselves know to be heer misaffirm'd" (p. 338). Milton insists that this truth needs no reinforcement but is simply sent out "in the native confidence of her single self, to earn, how she can, her entertainment in the world, and to finde out her own readers; few perhaps, but those few, such of value and substantial worth, as truth and wisdom, not respecting numbers and bigg names, have bin ever wont in all ages to be contented with" (pp. 339–40).

Yet Milton's truth, like the king's, is embedded in and shaped by seventeenth-century politics. As an object of political debate and ideological struggle, such truth is not, in Foucault's words, "outside power, or lacking in power."[24] When, as confuter of Charles, Milton claims to be part of the "sole remainder" or remnant selected by God "to stand upright and stedfast in his cause; dignify'd with the defence of truth and public libertie" (p. 348), he politicizes not only martyrdom but also the truth to which martyrs bear witness. Later in the work, he more radically conflates truth with justice and claims both were operative in executing the king: "either Truth and Justice are all one, for Truth is but Justice in our knowledge, and Justice is but Truth in our practice ... or else, if there be any odds, that justice, though not stronger then truth, yet by her office is to put forth and exhibit more strength in the affaires of mankind" (pp. 583–84). Writing thus, Milton hopes to "set free the minds of English men from longing to returne poorly under the Captivity of Kings, from which the strength and supreme Sword of Justice hath deliverd them" (p. 585). Like the Royalists, Milton strives to appropriate and deploy justice and truth for his political cause: once again, it is clear that such truth is a thing of this world, produced and defined in ideological struggle.

Central to *Eikonoklastes*, then, is Milton's rebuttal of Charles's claim to cap the Foxean tradition of martyrdom. To Charles's false, theatrical martyrdom, Milton opposes his own witness to the truth, a revised and reconstituted kind of martyrdom. Ironically, after the Restoration, *Eikonoklastes* itself suffered the traditional fate of a martyr—public burning by the common hangman. But Milton was left alive to contemplate and develop new modes of witness, of standing upright for the truth.

V

After 1660, although Milton's "left hand" no longer produced polemical prose, he continued his fight against kingship in the more allusive medium of poetry. *Paradise Regained*, seemingly so remote from contemporary political issues, is centrally concerned with depicting a Christ who cannot be associated with the Stuart monarchy. Milton's Son of God recalls the *Eikon Basilike* and the martyrologies of Charles I precisely to critique the claims of one who suffers for the preservation of earthly monarchy.[25] If in *Eikonoklastes* Milton primarily sought to rewrite the figure of Charles so as to deny him martyrdom with Christ, in *Paradise Regained* he strives, even more radically, to rewrite the meaning of martyrdom. Milton constructs a Son of God who embodies many of the characteristics of Foxe's martyrs—constancy in affliction, plain speaking of the truth, self-composure. Yet the Son is no martyr in the traditional sense employed by Foxe and elaborated by Gauden and the martyrologies; he is a victor who does not die to achieve his conquest. Rejecting the theatrical suffering and lachrymose exaltation of the recent English royal martyr, Milton reinvents in *Paradise Regained* the root sense of martyrdom as witnessing to the truth. *Paradise Regained* counters the Royalist appropriation of the discourse of martyrdom by radically rewriting both recent English political history and the centuries-old literary and cultural tradition of the royal martyr.

The long-standing problems of the poem are significant with regard to this revisionary project. The Son of God in *Paradise Regained* has been termed a "celibate detective," "heartless, prissy, or downright cold," a "peevish obscurantist," and an "inhuman snob."[26] The Son refuses to act or even to show any emotion. Faced with its spare style, austere setting, and paucity of action, readers have found the poem, as well as its hero, baffling and cold.²⁷ Even the most basic questions remain unsettled. Why this Subject? Why not the crucifixion? Is there development? Does the Son learn anything? Is there a miracle atop the temple tower? Why does Satan fall astonished? Such cruxes are not resolved by classifying the poem as brief epic. Indeed, Milton's rise of that genre is equally puzzling. Why no heroic action, figurative richness, poetic allusiveness, divine intervention?²⁸

Viewing *Paradise Regained* as participating in the political discourse of martyrdom clarifies a number of these issues. Here epic action, narrative, and plot are circumscribed by the single action of the martyr who must speak the truth—repeatedly, constantly. The hero's actions consist precisely in his witness to the truth—speaking out, enduring fraud and force, standing upright to the end. Divine intervention comes by way of the inward consolations which fortify martyrs. Epic allusiveness and figurative richness become Satanic snares, pitfalls to the plain and simple truth. While the Royalist tracts focus on the passion and crucifixion of Christ with only scant attention to the wilderness temptation as preparation for Christ's martyrdom, for Milton the temptation not only prepares for but essentially replaces the passion and crucifixion. Paradise is regained not by theatrical suffering but by an intellectual debate in the wilderness; the genre is not tragedy but brief epic, the protagonist not the crucified, kingly Christ but the constant, unmoved Son of God.

Unlike the Royalist martyrologies, *Paradise Regained* offers no physical suffering and death, no pathos, no public spectacle, no weeping audience. The poem is deliberately antitheatrical, or, rather, it links theatricality with Satan, who has a full complement of props, costumes, scenery, and dramatic ploys. While Satan seems to do all the acting, he also continually presses the Son to say or do something dramatically interesting.²⁹ The character of the Son—private, terse, unemotional—is the opposite of that of the king, who acts out a well-calculated pageant before a gullible audience. The Royalists may have the theater, but Milton has the truth.

The contemporary political discourse which linked Charles Stuart with Christ thus clarifies both Milton's choice and treatment of his subject in *Paradise Regained*. There is, to begin with, the simple, essential, but continually overlooked point that the hero of *Paradise Regained* is never called Christ. He is the "Son of God" (thirty-six times), the "Son" (fifteen times), "our Saviour" (eighteen times), "Jesus" (five times), "Messiah" (seven times), but never Christ, the one in whom the kingly line of David had been fulfilled.[30] Critics, however, invariably call this character Christ, thus coloring the character and poem with the sacramental associations of earthly kingship which Milton consciously avoided. The Christ of the Gospels is dramatically attractive as he suffers for others, forgives and prays for his enemies. The passion of Christ is central in the Gospels, and it was the language of the passion narratives which Charles so powerfully appropriated. Christ's passion takes place in the capital, Jerusalem; his agony in the garden, trial, condemnation, and carrying of the cross are all publicly accessible events. The Christ of the Gospels does not eschew the notion of kingship, although he also states, paradoxically, that "My kingdom is not of this world" (John 18:36, King James Version). Charged before Pilate with claiming to be the king of the Jews, Christ simply replies, "Thou sayest it" (Matt. 27:11; Mark 15:2; Luke 23:3).[31] The passion of the gospel Christ is compelling because of the pathos he evokes as a figure tragically misunderstood and unjustly put to death. What Milton leaves out of a poem on paradise regained is, from this perspective, astonishing. In rejecting the passion narratives as models for telling how Christ regains paradise, Milton represses the main emphases of the Gospels—Christ misunderstood, suffering for others, redeeming humanity through his death and resurrection. The witness of Milton's Son of God counters and challenges the pathos and dramatic appeal not only of the martyred Charles but also of the Christ whom Charles imitates.

Suffering and death, the traditional marks of martyrdom, are invoked in *Paradise Regained*, but then only to be pushed beyond the margins of the narrative. God the Father explains the Son's future mission: "To conquer Sin and Death the two grand foes, / By Humiliation and strong Sufferance: / His weakness shall o'ercome Satanic strength / And all the world, and mass of sinful flesh" (1.159–62). The Son knows from the beginning that his claim to his promised kingdom will ultimately consist in a traditional martyr's witness: "my way must lie / Through many a hard assay even to the death, / Ere I the promis'd Kingdom can attain" (1.263–65). Satan, too, forecasts the Son's future suffering and death: "Sorrows, and labors, opposition, hate, / Attends thee, scorns, reproaches, injuries, / Violence and stripes, and lastly cruel death" (4.386–88). Rejecting an earthly kingship, the Son envisages his God-appointed mission thus:

> What if he hath decreed that I shall first
> Be tried in humble state, and things adverse,
> By tribulations, injuries, insults,
> Contempts, and scorns, and snares, and violence,
> Suffering, abstaining, quietly expecting
> Without distrust or doubt, that he may know
> What I can suffer, how obey? who best
> Can suffer, best can do; best reign, who first
> Well hath obey'd.
>
> [3.188–96]

While the Son's rejoinder to Satan here seems to refer to future martyrdom, his speech (which significantly omits any mention of the crucifixion) also strikingly describes the action of *Paradise Regained* itself. In a very material sense, the wilderness temptation—during which the Son is tried by "injuries, insults, / Contempts, and scorns, and snares, and violence" and responds by "Suffering, abstaining, quietly expecting / Without distrust or doubt"—substitutes for traditional martyrdom in Milton's poem. The Son's suffering here consists of endurance as he abstains from earthly political power. Martyrdom thus delineated can encompass all the faithful republicans in Restoration England (including those who do not bear the ultimate witness of death). In Milton's hands, the martyrdom of the Son of God becomes an inclusive condition, no longer unique and no longer linked with his kingship—or with that of Charles I.

Although the Son does not suffer death in *Paradise Regained*, he nonetheless shows throughout his temptations the constancy which centrally defines Foxean martyrs. This, however, has been perhaps his most frustrating and puzzling trait for readers. In response to Satanic temptations, the Son replies "sternly" (1.406), "with unalter'd brow" (1.493), "temperately" (2.378), "patiently" (2.432), "calmly" (3.43), "fervently" (3.121), "unmov'd" (3.386, 4.109), "with disdain" (4.170), and "sagely" (4.285). During the Satanic storm he is "patient" (4.420), "Unshaken" (4.421), and "unappall'd" (4.425). Satan names the trait that constitutes the Son's central defense when he rejects Belial's suggestion of a temptation involving women: "with manlier objects we must try / His constancy" (2.225–26). The simile which opens book 4 of *Paradise Regained* recalls the frontispiece to *Eikon Basilike* as well as Charles's claims (repeated by the martyrologies) of his constancy in faith through storms of popular rage: "[As] surging waves against a solid rock, / Though all to shivers dash't, th' assault renew, / Vain batt'ry, and in froth or bubbles end; / So Satan" (4.18–21).[32] Likewise, Satan later complains that he has found the Son "Proof against all temptation as a rock / Of Adamant, and as a Center, firm" (4.533–34). This constancy reaches its apex (literally and dramatically) in *Paradise Regained* in the temptation of the Tower, when the Son stuns Satan by the untheatrical action of standing still: "To whom thus Jesus. Also it is written, / Tempt not the Lord thy God; he said and stood / But Satan smitten with amazement fell" (4.560–62).

And yet, as Milton himself had argued in *Eikonoklastes*, such constancy is in itself insufficient. Milton wants to show that the Son of God, unlike Charles, is constant in his witness to the truth. The Son declares early in *Paradise Regained* that even as a child he felt himself "born to promote all truth, / All righteous things" (1.205–6). Military might allures him to subdue tyrannic power to these specific ends: "Till truth were freed, and equity restor'd" (1.220). By contrast, Satan is repeatedly defined in terms of falsehood. The Son reproaches Satan as "compos'd of lies / From the beginning, and in lies wilt end" (1.407–8). Later, he charges Satan: "For lying is thy sustenance, thy food. / Yet thou pretend'st to truth" (1.429–30). Even Satan praises (though guilefully) the Son's truthfulness: "Hard are the ways of truth, and rough to walk, / Smooth on the tongue discourst, pleasing to th' ear, / And tunable as Silvan Pipe or Song; / What wonder their if I delight to hear / her dictates from thy mouth?" (1.478–82). This praise is blandishment offered as a response to the Son's characterization of himself in terms of truth:

> God hath now sent his living Oracle
> Into the World to reach his final will,
> And sends his Spirit of Truth henceforth to dwell
> In pious Hearts, an inward Oracle
> To all truth requisite for men to know.
> [1.460–64]

Truth, as embodied in the Son, becomes inward, not visible, not subject to display. Such a definition is politically charged, formed in a nexus of political struggle. Thus *Paradise Regained* dissociates truth from kingship, as the Son confirms his unlikeness to Charles by rejecting an earthly throne and redefining kingship: "But to guide Nations in the way of truth / By saving Doctrine, and from error lead / To know, and knowing worship God aright, / Is yet more Kingly" (2.473–76). Once the Son has definitively denied any association with earthly political power, the narrator concludes: "So spake Israel's true King, and to the Fiend / Made answer meet, that made void all his wiles. / So fares it when with truth falsehood contends" (3.441–43).

Finally, as opposed to Charles's false kingly witness, the Son's true witness is private. While Charles courts publicity as a martyr, publishing his meditations and seeking through theatrics to rouse the people, Milton's Son of God is alone in the wilderness. Milton moves his hero's public role—not only his suffering and death, but his entire ministry—beyond the poem's purview. Although it opens with the public baptism of the Son, the action then relocates to a private sphere. Unlike Charles, Milton's Son of God is found "tracing the Desert wild, / Sole, but with holiest Meditations fed" (2.109–10). Satan mocks the Son's circumstances—"Thou art unknown, unfriended, low of birth, / A Carpenter thy Father known, thyself / Bred up in poverty and straits at home; / Lost in a Desert here and hunger-bit" (2.413–16)—and tempts him to seek fame: "These Godlike Virtues wherefore dost thou hide? / Affecting private life, or more obscure / In savage Wilderness" (3.21–23). But the Son harshly rejects public acclaim, the "people's praise," in language which strikingly recalls Milton's earlier polemic against the "herd" in *Eikonoklastes*: "And what the people but a herd confus'd, / A miscellaneous rabble, who extol / Things vulgar, and well weigh'd, scarce worth the praise?" (3.49–51). The link with Milton's *Eikonoklastes* clarifies the otherwise puzzling severity of these lines. Milton's Son of God, unlike Charles, rejects popular fame because he witnesses not to himself but to God: "Shall I seek glory then, as vain men seek / Oft not deserv'd? I seek not mine, but his / Who sent me, and thereby witness whence I am" (3.105–7).

The human bystanders in *Paradise Regained* neither see nor hear about the Son's temptation in the wilderness. Andrew and Simon are disappointed and baffled by the Son's disappearance; nonetheless they summon up their faith: "But let us wait; thus far he hath perform'd, / Sent his Anointed, and to us reveal'd him, / By his great Prophet, pointed at and shown, / In public" (2.49–52). Mary is not present at the baptism but hears by report that her son, "Private, unactive, calm, contemplative" (2.81), has now been "acknowledg'd ... / By *John* the

Baptist, and in public shown, / Son own'd from Heaven by his Father's voice" (2.83–85). Apprehensive about her son—"But where delays he now? Some great intent / Conceals him" (2.95–96)—Mary too keeps faith: "But I to wait with patience am inur'd" (2.102). The poem hence provides a model for the faithful few in Milton's Restoration audience, as the poet conceived them and his hero alike. The Son's true witness never finds a human audience in the poem. After withstanding Satanic temptation, the Son simply goes home: "hee unobserv'd / Home to his Mother's house private return'd" (4.638–39).

Yet the Son is not wholly unobserved for he has, in the first place, a divine audience. God the Father explains that he is sending the Son

> That all the Angels and Ethereal Powers,
> They now, and men hereafter, may discern
> From what consummate virtue I have chose
> This perfect Man, by merit call'd my Son,
> To earn Salvation for the Sons of men.
> [1.163–67]

Satan too, of course, closely tracks the Son's witness and is ultimately stunned and defeated by it. Finally, the Son is not unobserved because Milton himself publishes as he textualizes the Son's "private" witness in the wilderness. The narrator will "tell of deeds / Above Heroic, though in secret done, / And unrecorded left through many an Age, / Worthy t' have not remain'd so long unsung" (1.14–17). In order to lodge his insistence that the true Son of God has no real earthly audience, Milton must speak to some earthly audience. This audience might be those few of "value and substantial worth" with whom, in *Eikonoklastes*, Truth is contented. For Milton, the very inaccessibility of *Paradise Regained* throughout its reception history, its lack of drama and popular appeal, would paradoxically confirm the truth of his discourse.

Paradise Regained thus inscribes a specifically Miltonic witness to the truth in the context of popular reaction to the crisis of Stuart monarchy. Charles's assimilation of himself to the Christ of the Gospels—suffering for the people and unjustly put to death—was so brilliantly successful that Milton could no longer use this discourse. In a number of ways *Paradise Regained* shares the mission of *Eikonoklastes*, but, instead of deconstructing the martyr King Charles, the poem deconstructs the Christ of the Gospels. *Paradise Regained* is not an orthodox work, no matter how much critics downplay its manifold difficulties. Milton's highly politicized redaction of the temptation of Christ in the wilderness, fully implicated in the contemporary politics of martyrdom, might be better named the (new) gospel according to John.

Notes

1. Matthew Henry Lee, ed., *Diaries and Letters of Philip Henry* (London, 1882), p. 12.

2. For general accounts of Charles's life and death, see C. V. Wedgwood, *A Coffin for King Charles* (New York, 1964); and John Bowle, *Charles I: A Biography* (London, 1975). On the civil war controversies, see Merritt Y. Hughes, intro. to *The Complete Prose Works of John Milton*, ed. Don Wolfe et al., 8 vols. (New Haven, Conn., 1953–82), 3:1–189.

3. "An Act of the Commons of England assembled in Parliament for erecting of a High Court of Justice for the Trying and Judging of Charles Steward King of England" (London, January 6, 1649), reprinted in *The Trial of King Charles the First*, ed. J. G. Muddiman (London, 1929), app. A, p. 193.

4. Michel Foucault, *Discipline and Punish: The Birth of the Prison*, trans. Alan Sheridan (New York, 1979). Clearly, Foucault's argument regarding the display of punishment is also altered when the king himself is the subject of punishment.

5. "King Charls, His Case, or an Appeal to all Rational men Concerning his Tryal at the High Court of Justice Being for the most part that which was intended to have been delivered at the Bar, if the King had pleaded to the Charge and put himself upon fair Tryal," (London, 1649), reprinted in Muddiman, ed., app. C, p. 234.

6. Ibid.

7. *A perfect Narrative of the whole Proceedings of the High Court of Justice, in the Trial of the King ... Published by Authority, to prevent false and impertinent Relations* (London, January 20–27, 1649), in Thomas Bayly Howell, *A Complete Collection of State Trials*, 33 vols. (London, 1816–26), 4:998.

8. Foucault, *Discipline and Punish*, p. 46.

9. Howell, 4:1138–41. A number of contemporary newspapers reported extensively on Charles's trial and execution, most following *A Perfect Narrative* almost verbatim. These newspapers, dated in the

Thomason tracts from January–February 1649, include *The Perfect Weekly Account, The Moderate Intelligencer, The Kingdomes Faithful Scout, The Kingdomes Weekly Intelligencer,* and *The Moderate.* Bruce Boehrer points astutely to the theatrical nature of Charles's execution in "Elementary Structures of Kingship: Milton, Regicide, and the Family," *Milton Studies* 23 (1987): 97–98.

10. Lee (n. 1 above), p. 12.

11. *Mercurius Elencticus* (London, 1649), reprinted in *A History of English Journalism to the Foundation of the Gazette,* ed. J. B. Williams (London, 1908), app. A, p. 205.

12. Quoted in introd., *Eikon Basilike,* ed. Philip Knachel (Ithaca, N.Y., 1966), p. xxxii. Knachel discusses the vexed question of the authorship of the "King's Book" in this introduction. All quotations from *Eikon Basilike* are from this edition and are noted parenthetically in my text.

13. Foxe's *Acts and Monuments of these latter and perilous days, touching matters of the church ... from the year of Our Lord a thousand to the time now present,* popularly known as the "Book of Martyrs," was first published in English in 1563 and frequently reprinted; after 1570 a copy was placed with the Bible in every English church. On the enormous influence of Foxe, see William Haller, *Foxe's Book of Martyrs and the Elect Nation* (London, 1963). The influence of Foxe on the *Eikon Basilike* is discussed by Florence Sandler, "Icon and Iconoclast," in *Achievements of the Left Hand: Essays on the Prose of John Milton,* ed. Michael Lieb and John T. Shawcross (Amherst, Mass., 1974), pp. 160–62; and John Knott, Jr., "'Suffering for Truths Sake': Milton and Martyrdom," in *Politics, Poetics, and Hermeneutics in Milton's Prose,* ed. David Loewenstein and James G. Turner (Cambridge, 1990), pp. 159–62.

14. For Foxe and the imperial tradition, see Janel Mueller, "Embodying Glory: The Apocalyptic Strain in Milton's *Of Reformation,*" in Loewenstein and Turner, eds., pp. 15–16.

15. See Helen Randall, "The Rise and Fall of a Martyrology: Sermons on Charles I," *Huntington Library Quarterly* 10 (1947): 135–67.

16. *An Elegie Upon the Death of Our Dread Soveraign Lord King* CHARLS *the* MARTYR (London, 1649), n.p. The martyrologies which I am citing are found in *Pamphlets, Books, Newspapers, and Manuscripts relating to the Civil War, the Commonwealth, and Restoration, Collected by George Thomason, 1640–1661* (British Library).

17. The Bishop of Downe, *The Martyrdom of King Charls I: Or his Conformity with Christ in his Sufferings: In a Sermon preached at Bredah, Before his Sacred Majesty King Charls the Second* (The Hague, 1649; reprint, London, 1660), p. 16.

18. *A Deepe Groane Fetch'd At the Funerall of that Incomparable and Glorious Monarch, Charles the First, King of Great Britaine, France and Ireland, &c, On Whose Sacred Person was acted that execrable, horrid & prodigious Murther* (London, 1649), p. 3.

19. *A Hand-Kirchife for Loyall Mourners or a Cordiall for Drooping Spirits, Groaning for the bloody murther, and heavy losse of our Gracious King, Martyred by his owne Trayterous and Rebellious Subjects* (London, 1649), pp. 5–6.

20. *The Scotch Souldiers Lamentation Upon the Death of the most Glorious and Illustrious Martyr, King Charles* (London, 1649), p. 18.

21. Anthonie Sadler, *The Loyall Mourner, Shewing the Murdering of King Charles the First: Fore-shewing the Restoring of King Charles the Second* (London, 1660), pp. 2–3.

22. *Eikonoklastes*, in Wolfe et al., eds. (n. 2 above), 3:365. Further references are included parenthetically in my text.

23. For a fuller discussion of Milton's attack on theatricality in *Eikonoklastes*, see Lana Cable, "Milton's Iconoclastic Truth," in Loewenstein and Turner, eds. (n. 13, above), pp. 143–45; and David Loewenstein, *Milton and the Drama of History: Historical Vision, Iconoclasm, and the Literary Imagination* (Cambridge, 1990), chap. 3.

24. "Truth and Power," in *Power/Knowledge: Selected Interviews & Other Writings by Michel Foucault*, ed. Colin Gordon et al. (New York, 1980), p. 131.

25. Recent critics have variously explored the political significance of *Paradise Regained*. Christopher Hill sees Christ as rejecting those things which led the revolutionaries astray; see his *Milton and the English Revolution* (New York, 1977), pp. 413–27. Andrew Milner argues that Christ's rejection of Satan's political offers reflects Milton's own quietism in face of the collapse of the Commonwealth (*John Milton and the English Revolution* [Totowa, N.J., 1981], pp. 167–79). Michael Wilding also finds quietism in the poem (*Dragon's Teeth: Literature in the English Revolution* [Oxford, 1987], pp. 249–53). David Quint argues that the poem challenges the Davidic claims of Charles I and II ("David's Census: The Politics of *Paradise Regained*," in *Re-membering Milton: Essays on the Texts and Traditions*, ed. Mary Nyquist and Margaret

Ferguson [New York and London, 1987], pp. 128–47). My own essay, which implicitly counters the claims of quietism, is indebted to John Knoll's brief but compelling discussion of *Paradise Regained* (n. 13 above), pp. 166–68.

26. See John Carey, *Milton* (London. 1969), p. 137; Alan Fisher, "Why Is *Paradise Regained* So Cold?" *Milton Studies* 14 (1980): 206; and Northrop Frye, "The Typology of *Paradise Regained*," in *Milton: Modern Essays in Criticism*, ed. Arthur E. Barker (London, 1965), p. 439.

27. See, e.g., Fisher. For a challenge to this view, see Wayne Anderson, "Is *Paradise Regained* Really Cold?" *Christianity and Literature* 34, no. 4 (Summer 1983): 15–23.

28. For a full account of the history and nature of brief epic, see Barbara Lewalski, *Milton's Brief Epic* (Providence, R.I., 1966).

29. From a different perspective, and without exploring the political implications, Stanley Fish has examined the antitheatrical nature of *Paradise Regained* in "The Temptation of Plot in *Paradise Regained*," *Milton Studies* 17 (1983): 163–85, and Inaction and Silence: The Reader in *Paradise Regained*," in *Calm of Mind: Tercentenary Essays on "Paradise Regained" and "Samson Agonistes" in Honor of John S. Diekhoff*, ed. Joseph Anthony Wittreich, Jr. (Cleveland, 1971), pp. 25–47.

30. *John Milton: Complete Poems and Major Prose*, ed. Merritt Y. Hughes (Indianapolis, 1957). Further references are included parenthetically in my text.

31. Christ's reply to Pilate in the Gospel of John is strikingly different: "Thou sayest that I am a king. To this end was I born, and for this cause came I into the world, that I should bear witness unto the truth. Every one that is of the truth heareth my voice" (John 18:37). Interestingly enough, while Milton's Son of God seems closest to this Christ, the Gospel of John has no temptation account. Milton seems to meld the Christ of the Gospel of John with the temptation episode found in the other Gospels.

32. On the connection with *Eikon Basilike*, see Knott, p. 167.

Chronology

1608	Milton is born in London on December 9.
1617	Enters St. Paul's School in London.
1625	Enters Christ's College at Cambridge.
1629	Completes his undergraduate studies.
1632	Completes his graduate studies.
1632-38	Studies at his parents' home.
1634	Writes *Comus* to be performed at Ludlow Castle.
1638-39	Visits Italy.
1641	Publishes *Of Reformation in England*.
1642	Publishes *The Reason of Church-Government*; marries Mary Powell, who returns to her parents soon after the marriage.
1643	Publishes *The Doctrine and Discipline of Divorce*.
1644	Publishes *Areopagitica*.
1645	Mary returns to her husband in London; he publishes *Poems of Mr. John Milton, Both English and Latin*.
1649	Publishes *The Tenure of Kings and Magistrates*; becomes Latin Secretary for Cromwell's Council of State.
1651	Publishes *Defense of the English People*.
1652	Becomes blind; his wife and son die.
1656	Marries Katherine Woodcock.
1658	His second wife and infant daughter die.

1660	Publishes *The Ready and Easy Way to Establish a Free Commonwealth*.
1663	Marries Elizabeth Minshull.
1667	Publishes *Paradise Lost*.
1671	Publishes *Paradise Regained* and *Samson Agonistes*.
1674	Publishes a revised version of *Paradise Lost*; Milton dies in November.

Works by John Milton

A Maske Presented at Ludlow Castle, 1634 (Comus). 1637.
Epitaphium Damonis. c. 1640.
Animadversions upon the Remonstrants Defence, against Smectymnuus. 1641.
Of Prelatical Episcopacy, and Whether It May Be Deduc'd from the Apostolical Times. 1641.
An Apology against a Pamplet Called A Modest Confutation of the Animadversions upon the Remonstrant against Smectymnuus. 1642.
The Reason of Church-Government Urg'd against Prelaty. 1642.
The Doctrine and Discipline of Divorce. 1643.
Areopagitica: A Speech for the Liberty of Unlicenc'd Printing. 1644.
The Judgment of Martin Bucer, concerning Divorce (translator). 1644.
Of Education. 1644.
Colasterion: A Reply to a Nameless Answer against The Doctrine and Discipline of Divorce. 1645.
Poems, Both English and Latin. 1645.
Tetrachordon: Expositions upon the Foure Chief Places in Scripture. 1645.
Eikonoklastes: In Answer to a Book Intitul'd Eikon Basilike. 1649.
The Tenure of Kings and Magistrates. 1649.
Pro Populo Anglicano Defensio (*In Defense of the English People*). 1651.
Pro Populo Anglicano Defensio Secunda. 1654.

Pro Se Defensio contra Alexandrum Morum. 1655.

The Cabinet-Council. 1658.

Considerations Touching the Likeliest Means to Remove Hirelings out of the Church. 1659.

A Treatise of Civil Power in Ecclesiastical Causes. 1659.

Brief Notes upon a Late Sermon, Titl'd, The Fear of God and the King *by Matthew Griffith.* 1660.

The Readie and Easy Way to Establish a Free Commonwealth. 1660.

Paradise Lost. 1667, 1674.

Accedence Commenc't Grammar. 1669.

The History of Britain. 1670.

Paradise Regain'd; to Which Is Added Samson Agonistes. 1671.

Artis Logicae Plenior Institutio. 1672.

Of True Religion, Haeresie, Schism, Toleration, and What Best Means May Us'd against the Growth of Popery. 1673.

Poems, &c., upon Several Occasions. 1673.

A Declaration. 1674.

Epistolarum Familiarum Liber Unus. 1674.

Literae Pseudo-Senatus Anglicani. 1676.

Character of the Long Parliament. 1681.

A Brief History of Moscovia. 1682.

Republican-Letters. 1682.

Letters of State, from the Year 1649 till the Year 1659. 1694.

Poetical Works. Ed. Patrick Hume. 1695.

Works. 1697.

Original Letters and Paper of State Addressed to Oliver Cromwell. Ed. John Nickolls. 1743.

De Doctrina Christiana Libri Duo. Ed. Charles Richard Sumner. 1825.

Works about John Milton

Achinstein, Sharon. *Milton and the Revolutionary Reader.* Princeton, N.J.: Princeton University Press, 1994.

Allen, Don Cameron. *The Harmonious Vision: Studies in Milton's Poetry.* Baltimore: Johns Hopkins Press, 1970.

Aryanpur, Manoocher. "*Paradise Lost* and *The Odyssey.*" *Texas Studies in Literature and Language* Vol. IX, No. 2 (Summer 1976): 151-166.

Battersby, James L *Rational Praise and Natural Lamentation: Johnson, Lycidas, and Principles of Criticism* Rutherford: Fairleigh Dickinson University Press, 1979.

Berkeley, David Shelley. *Inwrought with Figures Dim. A Reading of Milton's "Lycidas."* The Hague; Paris: Mouton, 1974.

Bowra, C.M. *From Virgil to Milton.* London: Macmillan & Co. Ltd, 1945.

Brown, Cedric. *John Milton: A Literary Life.* New York: St. Martins, 1995.

Clay, Daniel. *Death in Milton's Poetry.* Lewisburg, Penn.: Bucknell University Press, 1994.

Cullen, Patrick. *Infernal Triad: The Flesh, the World, and the Devil in Spenser and Milton.* Princeton: Princeton University Press, 1975.

Davies, Stevie. *Images of Kingship in Paradise Lost : Milton's Politics and Christian Liberty.* Columbia : University of Missouri Press, 1983.

Driscoll, James P. *The Unfolding God of Jung and Milton.* Lexington: University Press of Kentucky, 1992.

Empson, William. *Milton's God*. Cambridge, U.K.; New York : Cambridge University Press, 1981.

Esterhammer, Angela. *Creating States: Studies in the Performative Language of John Milton and William Blake*. Toronto: University of Toronto Press, 1994.

Evans, J. Martin. *The Miltonic Moment*. Lexington: University Press of Kentucky, 1998.

Fallon, Robert Thomas. *Divided Empire: Milton's Political Imagery*. Philadelphia: Pennsylvania State University Press, 1995.

———. *Milton in Government*. Philadelphia: Pennsylvania State University Press, 1993.

Fish, Stanley Eugene. *Surprised by Sin: The Reader in Paradise Lost*. Berkeley: University of California Press, 1971.

———. *How Milton Works*. Cambridge, Mass.: Belknap Press of Harvard University Press, 2001.

Fletcher, Angus. *The Transcendental Masque: An Essay on Milton's Comus*. Ithaca, N.Y.: Cornell University Press, 1971.

Gallagher, Phillip J. *Milton, the Bible, and Misogyny*. Colombia: University of Missouri Press, 1990.

Hill, John Spencer. *John Milton, Poet, Priest, and Prophet: A Study of Divine Vocation in Milton's Poetry and Prose*. Totowa, NJ: Rowman and Littlefield, 1979.

Honeygosky, Stephen R. *Milton's House of God: The Invisible and Visible Church*. Colombia: University of Missouri Press, 1993.

Hyman, Lawrence W. *The Quarrel Within: Art and Morality in Milton's Poetry*. Port Washington, N.Y.: Kennikat Press, 1972.

Kolbrener, William. *Milton's Warring Angels: A Study of Critical Engagements*. London: University of Cambridge Press, 1997.

Krouse, F. Michael. *Milton's Samson and the Christian Tradition*. Princeton: Princeton Univ. Press, 1949.

Langford, Thomas. "The Temptations in *Paradise Regained*." *Texas Studies in Literature and Language*, Vol. IX, No. 1 (Spring 1967): 37-46.

Lawry, Jon S. *The Shadow of Heaven: Matter and Stance in Milton's Poetry*. Ithaca, N.Y.: Cornell University Press, 1968.

Leonard, John. *Naming in* Paradise Lost: *Milton and the Language of Adam and Eve*. Oxford: Oxford University Press, 1990.

Levi, Peter. *Eden Renewed: The Public and Private Life of John Milton*. New York: St. Martins, 1997.

Lewalski, Barbara K. *The Life of John Milton: A Critical Biography*. Oxford, UK ; Malden, MA : Blackwell Publishers, 2000.

Lewis, C.S. *Preface to Paradise Lost*. London: Oxford University Press, 1942.

Lieb, Michael. *Milton and the Culture of Violence*. Ithaca, NY: Cornell University Press, 1994.

Lieb, Michael, and John T. Shawcross, eds. *Achievements of the Left Hand: Essays on the Prose of John Milton*. Amherst: University of Massachusetts Press, 1974.

Loewenstein, David. *Milton: Paradise Lost*. London: Cambridge University Press, 1993.

Low, Anthony. *The Blaze of Noon: A Reading of Samson Agonistes*. New York: Columbia University Press, 1974.

Madsen, William G. *From Shadowy Types to Truth: Studies in Milton's Symbolism*. New Haven, Yale University Press, 1968.

Marjara, Harinder Singh. *Contemplation of Created Things: Science in Paradise Lost*. Toronto: University of Toronto Press, 1992.

Martz, Louis L. *Poet of Exile: A Study of Milton's Poetry*. New Haven, Yale University Press, 1980.

Miller, Leo. *John Milton's Writings in the Anglo-Dutch Negotiations, 1651-1654*. Pittsburgh, Penn.: Duquesne University Press, 1992.

Moore, Leslie E. *Beautiful Sublime: the Making of* Paradise Lost *1701-1734*. Stanford, NJ: Stanford University Press, 1990.

Mustazza, Leonard. *"Such Prompt Eloquence" : Language As Agency and Character in Milton's Epics*. Lewisburg : Bucknell University Press ; London ; Cranbury, NJ : Associated University Presses, 1988.

Nicolson, Marjorie. *John Milton: A Reader's Guide to His Poetry*. New York: Farrar, Straus, 1963.

Parker, William Riley and Gordon Campbell, eds. *Milton: A Biography*. New York: Clarendon Press, 1996.

Patterson, Annabel, ed. *John Milton*. New York: Addison-Wesley, 1992.

Patrides, C.A., ed. *Milton's Lycidas: The Tradition and the Poem*. New York: Holt, Rinehart and Winston, 1961.

Porter, William M. *Reading the Classics and* Paradise Lost. Lincoln: University of Nebraska Press, 1993.

Richmond, Hugh M. *The Christian Revolutionary: John Milton*. Berkeley: University of California Press, 1974.

Ricks, Christopher. *Milton's Grand Style*. Oxford: Oxford University Press, 1963.

Rosenblatt, Jason P. *Torah and Law in* Paradise Lost. Princeton, NJ: Princeton University Press, 1994.

Rushdy, Ashraf H. *The Empty Garden: The Subject of Late Milton*. Pittsburgh: University of Pittsburgh Press, 1992.

Rumrich, John P. *Milton Unbound: Controversy and Reinterpretation*. London: Cambridge University Press, 1996.

Schulman, Lydia Dittler. Paradise Lost *and the Rise of the American Republic*. Boston: Northeastern University Press, 1992.

Shawcross, John T. *John Milton: The Self and the World*. Lexington: University Press of Kentucky, 1993.

Shoaf, R. A. *Milton, Poet of Duality*. Gainseville: University Press of Florida, 1993.

Steadman, John M. *The Wall of Paradise: Essays on Milton's Poetics*. Baton Rouge : Louisiana State University Press, 1985.

———. *Moral Fiction in Milton and Spenser*. Colombia: University of Missouri Press, 1995.

Tanner, John S. *Anxiety in Eden: A Kierkegaardian Reading of Paradise Lost*. London: Oxford University Press, 1992.

Tayler, Edward W. *Milton's Poetry : Its Development in Time*. Pittsburgh: Duquesne University Press, 1979.

Thorpe, James Ernest. *John Milton: The Inner Life*. New York: H. E. Huntington, 1983.

Tuve, Rosemond. *Images and Themes in Five Poems by Milton*. Cambridge: Harvard University Press, 1957.

Werman, Golda. *Milton and Midrash*. Washington, D.C.: The Catholic University of America Press, 1995.

Womack, Mark. "On the Value of Lycidas." *Studies in English Literature*: 1500-1900, Vol. 37, No. 1, (Winter 1997): 119-136.

Wood, Derek N. C. *Exiled from Light: Divine Law, Morality, and Violence in Milton's* Samson Agonistes. Toronto; Buffalo: University of Toronto Press, 2001.

Zagorin, Perez. *Milton: Aristocrat and Rebel: The Poet and His Politics.* New York: Boydell & Brewer, 1992.

WEBSITES

The Classic Text: John Milton
www.uwm.edu/Dept/Library/special/exhibits/clastext/clspg117.htm

John Milton: The Milton-L Home Page
www.richmond.edu/~creamer/milton/

The John Milton Reading Room
www.dartmouth.edu/~milton/

The Milton Quarterly
www.ohiou.edu/milton/

Milton Society of America
www.uwm.edu/Library/arch/findaids/uwmss104.htm

Contributors

HAROLD BLOOM is Sterling Professor of the Humanities at Yale University and Henry W. and Albert A. Berg Professor of English at the New York University Graduate School. He is the author of over 20 books, including *Shelley's Mythmaking* (1959), *The Visionary Company* (1961), *Blake's Apocalypse* (1963), *Yeats* (1970), *A Map of Misreading* (1975), *Kabbalah and Criticism* (1975), *Agon: Toward a Theory of Revisionism* (1982), *The American Religion* (1992), *The Western Canon* (1994), and *Omens of Millennium: The Gnosis of Angels, Dreams, and Resurrection* (1996). *The Anxiety of Influence* (1973) sets forth Professor Bloom's provocative theory of the literary relationships between the great writers and their predecessors. His most recent books include *Shakespeare: The Invention of the Human*, a 1998 National Book Award finalist, and *How to Read and Why*, which was published in 2000. In 1999, Professor Bloom received the prestigious American Academy of Arts and Letters Gold Medal for Criticism.

ELLYN SANNA has authored more than 50 books, including adult non-fiction, novels, young adult biographies, and gift books. She also works as a freelance editor and manages Scrivener's Ink, an editorial service.

NEIL HEIMS is a freelance writer, editor and researcher. He has a Ph.D in English from the City University of New York.

T. S. ELIOT was one of the most distinguished literary figures of the twentieth century. While most famously know for *The Waste Land*, and "The Love song of J Alfred Prufrock," Eliot was also a respected literary critic.

STANLEY EUGENE FISH is the Dean of the College of Liberal Arts and Sciences at the University of Illinois at Chicago. Fish is considered to be one of the world's leading Milton scholars, and has written extensively in the fields of literary and cultural criticism.

LAURA LUNGER KNOPPERS is an Associate Professor of English at the Penn State University. Her recent works include *Historicizing Milton: Spectacle, Power, and Poetry in Restoration England and Constructing Cromwell: Ceremony, Portrait, and Print, 1645-1661*.

INDEX

Areopagitica, (pamphlet), 20–21, 52–53
  on censorship, 16

Bloom, Harold
  introduction of Milton, 1–5
Book of Martyrs, (Foxe), 120
  on true martyrdom, 115
Byrd, William
  Elizabethan composer, 36

Chariot of Wrath, (Knight)
Charles I
  compared to Christ, 118
  execution of, 111
  royal martyrdom, 113–114
  trial of 112
  on war, 14
Charles II
  return of, 24, 120
Chaucer, 1, 73
Civil War, 67, 71
Cromwell, Oliver
  his death, 24
  dissolved parliament, 22
  puritan leader, 16
  reformed English-Dutch alliance, 23
"Comus," (Pastoral Masque), 3, 66, 72
  content of, 11–12
  on evil, 46, 54

  the lady, 88, 91
  on reality, 44

Dante, 1, 63, 73
"Death of a Fair Infant, On,"
  written first year at Cambridge, 9
Defense of the English People, 25
Defense of Poetry, (Shelley), 47
Doctrine and Discipline of Divorce, The, 15
Dryden, 71, 78
  preserved language, 62

Education, On, 7, 15, 50
Eikon Basilike, "The Kings Book," 116, 121,123
  on Charles I, 18, 115
  his Charles I death, 112
  political ramifications, 120
Eikonoklastes, 25, 122–123, 127
  fame and son of God, 128–129
  rebuttal of *Eikon*, 120
Eliot, T.S.,
  blank verse, 77
  the English Language, 64, 78–79
  influence of Milton, 70–71
  on Milton's greatness, 57–58
  on Poetry and Poets, 57–79
  the practitioner, 65
  the scholar, 65

style of poetry, 72
syntax, 69, 74
on visual and auditory poetry, 62–63
on writing poetry, 67
English Civil War, 1
English Poems, (Williams)
criticism of Milton, 66
Empson, William, 38
Evelyn, John,
the great fire, 30

Faustus, Dr., 59
Fish, Stanley Eugene,
the choices, 86–97
the consequences, 97–103
the interpretative choice, 81–109
notes of, 103–109
on *Paradise Lost*, 81–103
vain speculations, 81–85
Frye, Northrop, 98

Gauden, John, 115
Graves, Robert, 38

Heaven and Earth, (Murray), 68
Heims, Neil,
Christine doctrine, 37
on good and evil, 47, 52
introduction to Milton, 35–56
on liberty, 35–36
Milton's faith of God, 49
notes of, 55–56
power of choice, 54
on sound, 39
understanding Milton, 35
on verse, 41
Hollander, John
on Milton's commentary, 39
Hyperion, (play), 69

Irene, (Johnson), 77
Ivory Tower, The, 61

James, Henry, 60–61
Johnson, Samuel, 65–66
his respect and style of poetry, 66
Joyce, James, 64
his styled compared to Milton, 62

Keats, 68–70
King Stephen, (play), 69
Knight, Wilson
on *Paradise Lost*, 75
Knoppers, Laura Lunger
on Charles II, 119–125
on Christ passion, 125
notes of, 130–133
Paradise Regained and the Politics of Martyrdom, 111–130
on trial and execution of Charles I, 112–115
the truth and Son of God, 127–128

"L' Allegro," (poem), 59
beginning of his writings, 2
pastoral poem, 9
Lawes, Henry, 11
performed music in "Comus," 3
Leavis, F. R., 39
Lewis, C. S. 45, 48
on *Paradise Lost*, 81–82
Life of Milton, (Johnson), 67
"Lycidas," 2
criticism of, 37
pastoral elegy, 3
political and private theme of, 12–13

Macbeth, 58–59
Masque, 11

Index

"Meditations upon Death"
  conclusion of *Eikon Basilike*, 117
Mercurius Elencticus, (newspaper), 114
Mercurius politicus, (Nedham), 21
"Midsummer Night's Dream, A,"
  (Shakespere), 3
Milton, John
  on Adam and Eve, 82–83
  Bible, the, 26
  his blindness, 19
  his death, 4, 34
  early life, 7
  the English language, 64
  Fall, the, 26
  family life, 10–11
  Italian Tour, 1
  as Latin Secretary, 20
  pamphlets, 14–15
  plague, 28–29
  political view, 67
  published manuscripts, 33
  on publishing *Paradise Lost*, 31
  religious beliefs, 10, 36–37
  return to England, 14
  on Son of God, 123
  his spirituality, 26
  struggle against monarchy, 1
  on style, 72
  of truth and justice, 122
  his verse, 41
Milton's Prosody, (Bridges), 76
Moderate, The, (Newspaper),
  Levellers, The, 21
Murray, Middleton
  on Keats, 68
  see also Heaven and Earth

"Nativity Ode, The," 44
Nedham, Marchamont, 21
Nicomachean Ethics, (Aristotle), 51

"On His Blindness," (Sonnet XIX),
  45
Oratorio...*The Creation*, (Haydn), 40

Paradise Lost, 33, 39, 40–47, 61–79
  Adams fall, 96–97
  the dream, 92–93
  on Eve's innocence, 91
  Eve's leaving, 99
  Eve and Satan, 47
  on The Fall, 34
  about God, 27
  on liberty and freedom, 36
  the prefix "dis," 43
  rival to *Illiad* and *Odyssey*, 4–5
  on temptation, 84, 102
  warning of Satan, 51
Paradise Regained, 4, 31–33, 44, 51
  Christ of the gospels, 125
  comparison of King Charles and
    Son of God, 127–128
  about good and evil, 52
  on Jesus, 35, 46
  martyrdom, 123–124
  on truth, 127–128
"Penseroso, II," 2, 3, 9
Pilgrims Progress, (Bunyan), 31
Pro Populo Anglicano Defensio, 18–19

"Rambler," (essay), Johnson, 76
*Ready and Easy Way to Establish a Free
  Commonwealth, The*, (pamphlet),
  24
Ricks', Christopher, 39

Samson, 74, 79
"Samson Agonistes," (play), 44, 46
  biblical story of, 29, 36
  faith of Milton, 49
  a great accomplishment, 4–5
  on publishing Milton's works, 33

Samson as a hero, 49
Samuel, Irene, 48
Sanna, Ellyn
   Biography of John Milton, 7–34
   accomplishes goal, 31
   on censorship, 16
   contemporary religious beliefs, 10
   developing his writing, 11
   his education, 7–9
   effects of Cromwell's death, 24–25
   fall of humanity, 26–27
   his marriage, 15–16
   on Mother's death, 12
   the new government, 18
   on *Paradise Regained*, 32–34
   on religious freedom, 17
   views of the press, 21
Shakespeare, 69
   comparison to Milton, 59–60
Simmons, Samuel
   published *Paradise Lost*, 31
"Song of Songs, The," (parody), 89

"Tempest, The," (Shakespeare), 3
"Tenure of Kings and Magistrates, The," (pamphlet)
   on power and the people, 17
Tillyard, Dr.
   on dissociation, 71
"True Religion Of," (pamphlet), 34

Ulysses, 62

Wife to Mr. Milton, (Graves), 38
"Winter's Tale, The," (Shakespeare), 3
"Work in Progress," 62, 64
Wotton, Sir Henry,
   proverb to Milton, 13